CAMBRIDGE
EXAMINATIONS
PUBLISHING

The Cambridge IELTS Course | **Vanessa Jakeman and Clare McDowell**

D0506691

Insight into IELTS

Updated edition

CAMBRIDGE
UNIVERSITY PRESS

PUBLISHED BY THE PRESS SYNDICATE OF THE UNIVERSITY OF CAMBRIDGE
The Pitt Building, Trumpington Street, Cambridge, United Kingdom

CAMBRIDGE UNIVERSITY PRESS
The Edinburgh Building, Cambridge CB2 2RU, UK
40 West 20th Street, New York, NY 10011–4211, USA
477 Williamstown Road, Port Melbourne, VIC 3207, Australia
Ruiz de Alarcón 13, 28014 Madrid, Spain
Dock House, The Waterfront, Cape Town 8001, South Africa

http://www.cambridge.org

First published 1999
Updated edition 2001
Seventh printing 2004

Printed in Dubai by Oriental Press

Text typeface Utopia 10.5/13pt.   *System* QuarkXPress®

ISBN 0 521 01148 5 Student's Book
ISBN 0 521 62660 9 Cassette

Cover design and graphic by Tim Elcock

Contents

THE WRITING MODULE

THE SPEAKING MODULE

SUPPLEMENTARY ACTIVITIES

IELTS PRACTICE TEST

Introduction

WHO IS THIS BOOK FOR?

Insight into IELTS has been designed as a course book for an IELTS preparation course. However, it is equally appropriate as a self-study resource book for students wishing to improve their IELTS skills on their own as it contains helpful advice, sample IELTS material throughout the units and detailed answer keys.

The book is appropriate both for learners seeking to enter an English-speaking university, school or college, as well as for people who may need to provide an IELTS score for the purposes of immigration to an English-speaking country. The book is targeted at students of approximately Band 6 level; however, the earlier units in each section are designed for lower-level learners or students not familiar with the IELTS test format, while the later units are intended to stretch the stronger candidates beyond their immediate IELTS needs and enhance their language skills overall.

CONTENT OF THE BOOK

The book consists of four parts:

- Listening, Reading, Writing and Speaking sections
- Supplementary activities for each unit
- A complete practice test
- Recording Script and Answer Key

Taken as a whole, the book contains ample classroom-based material within the units for a preparation course of between 40 and 50 hours. When used with the Supplementary activities which accompany each unit, the material will last much longer.

The first part of the book is divided into four sections: Listening, Reading, Writing and Speaking, to reflect the format of the test, and these are broken down into manageable units. Each section begins with an overview of the IELTS test and students who work their way through the book will become familiar with all question types and tasks that they are likely to meet in the test. The skills covered are not restricted to test-taking strategies alone but also reflect the broader range of language that students will encounter in an English-speaking environment, whether at university or in the wider community.

The units contain class and pair activities and the opportunity for individual practice. Teachers may choose to work systematically through each section, taking advantage of the graded approach, or, alternatively, select material to suit their learners' needs as required.

The Supplementary activities can be used to expand the units as follow-up work in class or as homework exercises. For students working on their own, they provide further opportunity to practise and consolidate the language covered in each unit or they can help students to structure their revision schedule once they have covered the units in the first part of the book.

The final part of the book offers a full practice IELTS test which is accompanied by a band conversion table (on page 189) to allow students to assess their approximate level in the Reading and Listening sections from their performance in this test.

A Recording Script is provided for the Listening units and the Listening part of the practice test and this is annotated to show where the answers are located in the text.

A thorough Answer Key is provided for all sections of the book, including the practice test. The Key provides a framework of support to ensure that students can receive feedback on all activities and exercises undertaken. It includes a selection of model Band 9 answers to a number of the writing questions. We would like to stress that these model answers represent only a sample of the many possible ways of approaching the writing tasks, but we hope that learners will find them a useful guide.

ABOUT THE TEST

There are two versions of the IELTS test.

Academic Module	General Training Module
for students seeking entry to a university or institution of higher education offering degree and diploma courses	for students seeking entry to a secondary school, to vocational training courses or for people taking the IELTS test for immigration purposes

Note: All candidates must take a test for each of the four skills: listening, reading, writing and speaking. All candidates take the same Listening and Speaking modules but may choose between the Academic or General Training versions of the Reading and Writing sections of the test. You should seek advice from a teacher or a student adviser if you are in any doubt about whether to sit for the Academic module or the General Training module.
The two do not carry the same weight and are not interchangeable.

TEST FORMAT

Listening
4 sections, 40 questions
30 minutes + 10 minutes transfer time

Academic Reading		General Training Reading
3 sections, 40 questions	OR	3 sections, 40 questions
60 minutes		60 minutes

Academic Writing		General Training Writing
2 tasks	OR	2 tasks
60 minutes		60 minutes

Speaking
11 to 14 minutes

Total test time
2 hours 55 minutes

The Listening Module

GENERAL LISTENING STRATEGIES

When you go to university you will have to interact with many different people in a number of situations. The IELTS Listening test is designed to reflect some of these real-world listening situations. The level of difficulty increases through the paper and there is a range of topics and tasks which test your comprehension skills, e.g. listening for specific information, such as dates and place names, listening for detail, understanding gist and understanding speaker attitude/opinion. As you work your way through the Listening units of this book, you will be introduced to a wide range of IELTS question types and additional exercises to help improve your overall listening strategies.

LISTENING FOR IELTS

Listening Test Format

Section 1: A conversation between two speakers in a social or semi-official context.

Section 2: A talk by a single speaker based on a non-academic situation.

Section 3: A conversation with up to four speakers based on academic topics or course-related situations.

Section 4: A university-style lecture or talk.

The Listening test is the first part of the IELTS examination and takes place at the beginning of the day. It takes about 40 minutes and consists of four recorded sections, each covering a different type of language and context. There are 10 questions in each section and you will be given time to read these questions before you listen to each part. As you will hear each recording _once only_ it is very important to understand exactly what you are being asked to do in each question. The question types vary and focus on a variety of different listening skills. For example, some questions involve completing a form, chart or diagram, others require you to select pictures which represent what you have heard. In addition there are note-taking exercises and multiple-choice questions. All aspects of the Listening test, as well as additional skills, are covered in this book.

Listening

- Who are the speakers?

- Where are they?

- Why are they speaking?

In order to understand what people are saying, it helps to know what their relationship is to each other and to you as the listener.

The language we choose to use will depend on our relationship to the other speakers, e.g. we use different language to talk to a family member as opposed to a teacher or a salesperson. Knowing the context of a conversation also helps us to understand the language because it helps us to anticipate what the speakers are going to talk about.

Pre-listening

- Look at the following pictures. Try to work out who the people are, where they are and why they are speaking to each other.
- Can you imagine what they are saying? Write some words in the speech balloons.

- How did you decide what the people were saying?
- Compare what you have written with your partner.

EXTRACT 1

- Listen to Unit 1, Extract 1. There are ten short conversations and one example. As you listen, complete the table to show *who* the speakers are and *why* they are speaking. The first one has been done as an example.

Conversation Number	Who are the speakers? (Relationship)	Why are they speaking? (Purpose)
Example	Customer/Sales assistant	Customer is asking where men's department is
1	customer / waiter	order food & wine
2	driver / police officer	traffic stop
3	David / wife	about recent traffic stop
4	Lecturer / teacher	lecture about world war
5	customer / receptionist	joining fee for Tennis club
6	student / Teacher	asking for extension on paper essay
7		essay
8		conversation re drinks
9		consultation w/ doctor
10		welcome by principal

 Follow-up: Spoken and written language

- Make a list of the types of language you hear spoken every day both in your own language and in English. Divide the list into two columns showing language which is spontaneous or unprepared and language which was probably written to be read out loud. Then discuss the questions below with a partner.

Unprepared spoken language
e.g. talking to family & friends
asking directions
....
....

Read out loud
radio news
....
....

11 What are the main differences between spoken language and language which was written to be read out loud? Is it harder to understand one than the other?

12 Why is it more difficult to understand people when they speak on the telephone? How is this similar to listening to a recorded conversation?

 For further practice, do the Supplementary activity on page 109.

Listening

UNIT 2 Listening for specific information

- What are the key words?

- What type of words are they?

Sometimes when we listen, we are only interested in finding out very specific information such as dates and times, names or key words.
It helps us to understand, if we can work out what kind of words we are listening for.

EXTRACT 1

- Look at the telephone message pad below. It comes from a house where a number of students live together.
- Discuss what information you need to listen out for in each message. If possible, write the type of word that is needed in the right-hand column.
- Listen to Unit 2, Extract 1 and complete the task.

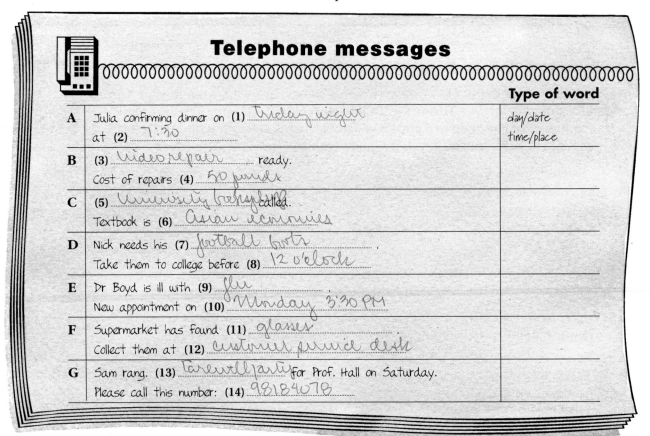

Telephone messages

		Type of word
A	Julia confirming dinner on **(1)** _friday night_ at **(2)** _7:30_	day/date time/place
B	**(3)** _video repair_ ready. Cost of repairs **(4)** _50 pounds_	
C	**(5)** _University bookshop_ called. Textbook is **(6)** _Asian economies_	
D	Nick needs his **(7)** _football boots_ . Take them to college before **(8)** _12 o'clock_	
E	Dr Boyd is ill with **(9)** _flu_ . New appointment on **(10)** _Monday 3:30 PM_	
F	Supermarket has found **(11)** _glasses_ . Collect them at **(12)** _customer service desk_	
G	Sam rang. **(13)** _farewell party_ for Prof. Hall on Saturday. Please call this number: **(14)** _98184078_	

EXTRACT 2

IELTS Listening Section 1	Table and note completion

How to approach the task

► In Section 1 of the IELTS Listening test you will hear a dialogue. One of the speakers may be seeking factual information such as names or dates which you will have to identify or note down. Alternatively you may have to select the right picture, fill in a form or complete some notes.

► Before you listen, look at the task below and decide what sort of information you are listening for.

► Answer the questions as you listen.

Questions 1–10

Complete the table and the notes below using **NO MORE THAN THREE WORDS** *for each answer.*

BLUE HARBOUR CRUISES

Name of cruise	Highlight Cruise	Noon Cruise	(1) Coffee Cruise
Price per person	$16	(4) $ 42	$25
Departure times	(2) 9:30 AM	12.00	(6) 2:15 P.M.
Included in the price	(3) souvenir postcard	(5) 3 course lunch	coffee and (7) sandwiches

Jetty No. 2 is situated (8) opposite shops
The commentary is in (9) English
The lady recommends that they (10) wear a hat

TEST TIP

You may find that a Listening section is divided into two parts.

EXTRACT 3

| IELTS Listening Section 1 | Form filling |

An IELTS Listening section will often contain more than one type of task, e.g. multiple choice and gap filling.

How to approach the task

► Look at the task below, which consists of a form with some information missing. Try to work out the possible context of the language from the task. Who could the speakers be? Why are they speaking?
► What role will you be playing when you complete the task? What sort of information will you be listening for?
► You only hear the extract once in the real test, so read the questions carefully *before* you listen.

Questions 1–10

Listen to the telephone conversation and complete the form below. Write **NO MORE THAN THREE WORDS OR A NUMBER** for each answer.

Golden Wheels CAR RENTALS

CUSTOMER REQUEST FORM

Customer's name (1) _Frank Moorcroft_

Address (2) _Flat 26, 19 Lakeroad Richmond_

Telephone (3) _36974500_

Driver's licence number (4) _UT9128_

Date for collection of vehicle (5) _23 rd June_

Circle the correct answer.

(6) Type of car chosen
  A small car
  B four-wheel drive
  C family car

(7) Number of days required
  A one day
  B three days
  C seven days

(8) Agreed cost per day
  A $50.00
  B $65.00
  C $70.00

(9) Pick up from
  A city
  B hotel
  C airport

(10) Method of payment
  A cheque
  B credit card
  C cash

Follow-up

- Look at the three forms below. Choose **one** and write a short dialogue to accompany it. Imagine that one of the speakers in your dialogue is asking questions and completing the form. Make sure that your dialogue includes enough information to allow the listener to complete the form.
- Read your dialogue to two other classmates. They must complete the form while they listen.

Campus Services
APPLICATION FOR PART-TIME WORK

Name of student ....

Address ....

....

Age ....

Work permit/tax file number ....

Experience/Qualifications ....

Type of work sought:
- Clerical
- Restaurant
- Other ....
- Taxi driving
- Telephone sales

The Key Language Centre
Student Enrolment Details

Name of student ....

Address ....

Nationality ....

Date of birth ....

Previous study (if any) ....

Length of course desired:
1 month   3 months   6 months   9 months

Type of accommodation desired:
Host family   Student hostel   University hall

Reason for studying English ....

....

Campus Sport
ENROLMENT FORM

Name ....

Address ....

....

University faculty ....

Student number ....

Type of membership required:
- Half-year
- Full-year
- Two-year
- Three-year
- Sports played ....

....

For further practice, do the Supplementary activity on page 109.

Listening

UNIT 3 Identifying detail

- When do we need to listen for detail?

- Why is detail important?

If someone is describing an object like an umbrella, it is the detail in the description, such as the colour or a reference to the shape, which allows us to differentiate it from another umbrella. So we need to listen carefully for the words which describe the detail.

Pre-listening

- Look at the pictures of the umbrellas, which are similar but not the same, and describe one to your partner. Is it clear which umbrella you are describing? These words may help you: *spots, stripes, handle, curved, straight, point, pointed*.

 EXTRACT 1

IELTS Listening Section 1	Multiple-choice pictures

How to approach the task

► Look at the task on the following page. In each case there is a question followed by three pictures. Try to work out the possible context of the language from the words in the questions and the pictures.

► Decide what information you should listen out for.

► Answer the questions as you listen.

Questions 1–6

Circle the appropriate letter.

Example What was Jill's job in Hong Kong?

TEST TIP

In Section 1 of the test only, you will hear the example played twice.

1 Which picture shows Gerry?

2 Where were Gerry and Sue married?

3 Which picture shows Sue's sister's children?

4 What time should Jill arrive for dinner?

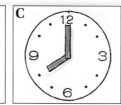  

5 What type of accommodation does Sue live in?

  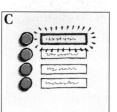

6 Which bell must you press?

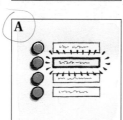 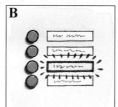 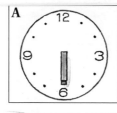

 For further practice, do the Supplementary activity on page 109.

Listening

UNIT 4 Identifying main ideas

- What are the speakers talking about?

- What are the main ideas and how are they developed?

When we take part in a conversation or listen to other people, we subconsciously separate the information that we need or that interests us from the rest of what we hear. In other words, we separate the main ideas from the supporting detail. Sometimes people use an introductory phrase to attract our attention and to give some clue to the topic.

 EXTRACT 1

- Look at the chart below. You will see that the situation and speakers have already been identified. Try to guess what the speakers *might say* from this information. This is not always possible. Why?
- Listen to Unit 4, Extract 1 and make a note of the words used by the first speaker to attract attention. Write this in the *Introductory phrase* column.
- Listen to the extract a second time and fill in the rest of the grid, briefly noting the *topic* and showing how the speakers *develop this topic*. The first one has been done for you as an example.

	Situation	Introductory phrase	Topic?	How does the topic develop?
Example	Two old school friends chatting	Guess who I saw today?	Meeting an old teacher	Talk about teacher's appearance
1	Department store: customer and sales assistant			
2	Husband and wife talking about the children			
3	Radio news item			
4	Two friends making plans for an outing			
5	Two students chatting in university canteen			
6	University librarian and student			
7	Sports equipment shop: assistant and two teenagers			
8	Vice Chancellor of a university speaking at a ceremony			

Follow-up

- Work with a partner. Select one of the pictures from the group of pictures below.
- Decide on a topic for the characters in the picture you have chosen.
- Write a short dialogue (4–5 lines) to accompany the picture. Try to write an appropriate introductory phrase or greeting for the first speaker.
- Act out the dialogue to two other classmates. Could they guess which picture it matches?

 EXTRACT 2

IELTS Section 2	**Multiple choice and note completion**

In Section 2 of the IELTS Listening test you will hear one person giving a talk on a topic of general interest. As well as listening for specific information, you may be asked to interpret the speaker's ideas. You will therefore need to follow the talk carefully and be prepared to separate the main ideas from the supporting detail.

How to approach the task

- ► Look at the questions below and try to work out from the vocabulary used what the topic is.
- ► Now read the questions carefully to find out what sort of information you need to listen out for.
- ► Underline in pencil the important words in the multiple-choice questions before you listen. This will help to focus your listening.
- ► Answer the questions as you listen.

Questions 1–5

Circle the correct answer.

1 The weekly radio programme is on
  A topics suggested by listeners.
  B local news items.
  C listeners' hobbies.

/ **2** The process of stamp production is
    A difficult.
    B expensive.
    ' **C** time consuming.

B **3** In the search for suitable subjects, people are invited to
    A research a number of topics.
    — **B** give an opinion on possible topics.
    / **C** produce a list of topics.

/ **4** Topics are sent for final approval to
    A a group of graphic artists.
    / **B** the Board of Directors.
    C a designers' committee.

C **5** Australian artists receive money
    / **A** only if the stamp goes into circulation.
    B for the design only.
    — **C** for the design and again if it is used.

Questions 6–8

*Complete the notes using **NO MORE THAN THREE WORDS** for each answer.*

Stamps must represent aspects of (6) ___national interest___

e.g. characters from literature or examples of wildlife.

There are no (7) ___living people___ *on Australian or*

British stamps.

A favourite topic in Britain is (8) ___kings & queens___

TEST TIP

When you transfer your answers to the answer sheet, make sure that you follow the same numbering as the questions on the question paper.

Questions 9–10

Circle the correct answer.

/ **9** The speaker says that
    A many people produce designs for stamps.
    B few people are interested in stamp design.
    / **C** people will never agree about stamp design.

B **10** The speaker suggests that
    A stamps play an important role in our lives.
    B too much attention is devoted to stamp production.
    / **C** stamps should reflect a nation's character.

 For further practice, do the Supplementary activity on page 110.

Listening

- What does the speaker mean exactly?

- How can we interpret intonation?

People do not always say exactly what they mean. As listeners we must learn to interpret the words people use as well as their intonation patterns. In this unit, we will investigate some ways of seeing beyond the surface meaning of spoken language while following a conversation.

Pre-listening

- Look at the following sentence: *I thought the assignment was due in on Thursday.*
- Try saying it in three different ways, to produce three different meanings.
  What are the three meanings? Discuss these with your partner.
- Try creating a similar short statement. See if you can vary the meaning by changing the word stress.
- Read your statements to your partner. Can you hear the differences in meaning?

EXTRACT 1

- Look at the chart below and note the headings of the different columns.
- Listen to Unit 5, Extract 1, which consists of an example and eight short, independent dialogues. As you listen, answer the focus question *Yes* or *No*.
- Discuss what indicators or language features helped you to interpret the real meaning of the speakers.

	Focus question	Yes/No	Indicators
Example	Did the woman like the shirt?	No	Her hesitation Rising intonation – uncertainty
1	Is the weather fine?	Yes	
2	Is the girl trying to avoid the date?	Yes	um hesitation
3	Was the man satisfied with the phone?	No	
4	Are university fees going to rise?	No	
5	Does the woman want to see the computer?	No	
6	Is the boy very sick?	No	
7	Did the woman like the movie?	Yes	
8	Is the teacher pleased with the boy's work?	No	

Pre-listening

- Look at the three posters advertising a student debate.
- Discuss what each of the posters means. Ask your teacher to explain their possible meaning if this is not clear. In these three cases, there are two possible sides to each argument.
- Make a list of things which could be said on either side of the argument for each poster. This will help you to understand Extract 2.
- Report back to the class.

 EXTRACT 2

In Section 3 of the IELTS Listening test you will have to follow a conversation with more than two speakers. In this extract you will hear a conversation between three friends who live in a student house together, Richard, Sue and Frank. They are having a conversation about how the government should spend public money. There are two tasks to accompany this listening extract.

Task 1

- Listen to the conversation. As you listen, complete the grid below by placing a ✓ in the box next to the name of the speakers each time they speak. Which of them speaks most often?

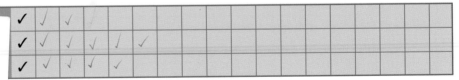

Task 2

- Now look at the questions below. Read them through carefully and underline any words that you think will help to focus your listening.
- Listen to the extract a second time and circle the correct answer for each question.

1 The person at the door is
  A looking for work.
  B asking for money.
  C looking for the hospital.
  D visiting her friends.

2 Frank thinks the hospital should be financed by
  A local residents.
  B a special health tax.
  C the state.
  D private companies.

3 Richard thinks Sue's view on hospital funding is
  A acceptable.
  B predictable.
  C uninteresting.
  D unreasonable.

4 Sue's attitude towards the government's spending is
  A disapproving.
  B indifferent.
  C understanding.
  D impartial.

5 Frank thinks that space research
  A is only for scientists.
  B is moving too slowly.
  C has practical benefits.
  D has improved recently.

6 In talking about space travel, Frank
  A displays his pessimism.
  B reveals an ambition.
  C makes a prediction.
  D refers to a book.

7 Sue thinks work is important because it
  A reduces the levels of crime.
  B gives individuals pride in themselves.
  C helps people find homes.
  D reduces the need for charity.

8 Richard's overall attitude is
  A helpful.
  B bitter.
  C disinterested.
  D sarcastic.

 For further practice based on this extract, do the Supplementary activity on page 110.

TEST TIP

In this type of task there are three speakers interacting and in the test you will only hear the conversation once. It is important that you are able to distinguish between the different speakers as well as understand what they are saying.

Listening

- What are 'signpost words'?

- How do they help us to understand?

Good public speakers and lecturers illustrate the stages of their talk through the use of 'signpost words'. Being able to identify and follow the signpost words will help you to understand formal spoken English.

Pre-listening

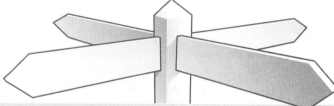

As with writing, speakers make use of special words to help introduce ideas and to provide a framework for what they are saying, especially in formal speech, such as a lecture or a talk. We can think of these words as 'signpost words' because they direct our listening; in other words, they warn us that more information is coming and suggest what kind of information this may be: e.g. additional, positive, negative, similar, different. They may also introduce examples of a main point made earlier.

- Look at the sample of unfinished 'spoken' text below. It starts with the signpost word *while*, which suggests that there is a contrast or opposite to follow.

> While a great deal has been achieved in the area of cancer research, there ...

This sentence could be completed with the words: ... *is still a lot we do not understand about cancer.*

Here are some possible 'directions' that the signpost words can take you in.
a Leading towards a comparison
b Leading towards a contrast or opposite
c Introducing an example of what was said earlier
d Suggesting cause and effect or result
e Providing additional information
f Setting out the stages of a talk

- First, read the sentences **1–10** on the next page and identify the signpost words and the direction (**a–f** above) that the words are taking you in. Then go on to the pair activity that follows.

1 Incoming governments often make promises which they cannot keep. For instance …

2 Every Roman town had at its centre a forum, where people came together to conduct their official and religious affairs. In addition, the forum …

3 The meteorological office predicted rain for the two weeks of the Olympic Games. In consequence, …

4 Learning a foreign language can be difficult and at times frustrating. However, …

5 Not only did the Second World War result in the displacement of millions of innocent civilians, it …

6 Despite the efforts of the government to reduce the incidence of smoking among teenagers and young adults, I regret to say that smoking …

7 This is how to approach writing an essay. First, you should read the question carefully. Then …

8 No matter how hard you try to justify the sport of fox hunting, the fact remains that …

9 Firstly I would like to talk about the early life of J. F. Kennedy. Secondly … and thirdly …

10 On the one hand, it may be advisable to study hard the night before an exam; on the other hand, …

- Try to complete the unfinished statements above by creating an ending which makes sense in each case, using the signpost words in the text to guide you.
- Read the finished texts out loud to your partner so that you can practise the intonation patterns which go with the signpost words. Make sure your voice rises and falls in the right places to reflect your intended meaning.

 EXTRACT 1

You can check the intonation patterns by listening to Unit 6, Extract 1, which gives some possible ways of completing the sentences.

EXTRACT 2

| IELTS Listening Section 3 | Note completion and labelling a diagram |

IELTS Section 3 Listening takes the form of a conversation between two or more people discussing an academic topic. Unlike the dialogues in Section 1, where the speakers are discussing everyday topics, Section 3 will require more careful attention to the conversation or argument being expressed. In the following example, you will hear an extract from a university tutorial with four speakers taking part. First look at the questions below and make sure you understand exactly what you have to label on the diagram.

Questions 1–3

Complete the notes. Use **NO MORE THAN THREE WORDS** *for each answer.*

ROVER ROBOT

The robot does the work of a (1) _Geologist_ . It looks like a (2) _microwave oven_ on wheels. It weighs 16.5 kg and travels quite (3) _slow_ .

Questions 4–7

Label the diagram of the rover robot.
Write **NO MORE THAN THREE WORDS** *for each answer.*

(4) _solar panels_

(6) _cameras_

(7) _aluminium_ wheels

(5) _warm box_

Questions 8–10

Complete the notes. Use **NO MORE THAN THREE WORDS** *for each answer.*

The rover cannot be steered in real time because of the
(8) _time delay_ .
Scientists decide on a (9) _course_ for the rover.
Mars is similar to Earth because it may have
(10) _water_ .

 For further practice, do the Supplementary activity on page 110.

Listening

UNIT 7 Being aware of stress, rhythm and intonation

- How do intonation and word stress help us to understand?

Public speakers and lecturers make use of stress, rhythm and intonation patterns, along with signpost words, to divide their information into 'chunks' of meaning. Learning to recognise these speech patterns will help you to understand formal spoken English whether you are listening to a live or a recorded talk.

Pre-listening

- Try saying the following telephone numbers. Notice how your voice goes up after each group and then drops as you come to the end of the whole number.

 5849 3714 *612 9983 4721 *01223 460278 *33 76 49 52 98 *0412 613612

Speakers normally use an upward intonation if they have more to add and let their voice drop when they come to the end of that piece of information.

EXTRACT 1

- Look at the five extracts below, taken from different lectures and mark in pencil the words which you think should be stressed and where your voice should rise and fall.
- Read the extracts out loud to your partner, as if you were giving a talk or a lecture, paying particular attention to the intonation patterns needed to keep the listener interested and to ensure that the meaning is clear. After you have both read each extract, listen to the recording and compare it with your versions.
- Try recording your own voice and then listen to yourself.

A
Urban society began when hunter-gatherers learnt (a) how to farm land, (b) how to domesticate animals and (c) how to build permanent structures to act as shelter.

B
There are three levels of government in Australia: firstly, there is Federal Government; then there is State Government and thirdly we have Local Government.

C
There are three levels of government in Australia: firstly, there is Federal Government, which looks after issues of national importance such as immigration and defence. Then there is State Government located in each capital city, and which has responsibility for such things as education, the police and urban and regional planning, and thirdly we find Local Government, which controls services such as waste collection, public libraries and childcare centres.

D
Was Napoleon poisoned or did he die of natural causes? The Napoleonic Society of America, an association of historians and collectors, has given a modern twist to this debate. They have done this by revealing the results of chemical analyses of hair said to have come from the head of the French emperor.

E
The many forms and styles of handwriting which exist have attracted a wide range of aesthetic, psychological and scientific studies, each with its own aims and procedures. Moreover, each of the main families of writing systems (European, Semitic, East Asian) has its own complex history of handwriting styles.

EXTRACT 2

IELTS Listening Section 4	Following a flow chart

Section 4 of the Listening test is always a lecture or a talk of some kind. In this example, you will hear the introduction to a lecture on child language acquisition. The speaker provides a framework for his talk using a number of signpost words.

How to approach the task

► Read the notes carefully to get an idea of the content and direction of the talk.
► Notice how the notes form part of a flow chart to reflect the format or organisation of the talk.

TEST TIP
If you need to use more than three words, the answer is probably incorrect.

Questions 1–10

*Complete the notes below. Use **NO MORE THAN THREE WORDS** for each answer.*

The Study of Child Language Acquisition

Example

● ......Fascinating.......... *because people have an* (1) ......*interest*...... *in children's learning*

● (2) ......*important*...... *because it leads to greater understanding of language*

● (3) ......*complex*...... *because of the difficulties encountered*

Part 1 of talk

Discussion of (4) ......*research methods*...... ▸ *includes the use of diaries, recordings and tests*

(5) ......*Language learning process*......

Speech in infants under one year – child becomes aware of own language	Speech in children under 5 years – linguistic (6) ......*ability*...... *analysis* becomes possible

Part 2 of talk

(7) ......*Awareness*...... *educational approaches* to development of linguistic skills

● Teaching (8) ......*Spoken*...... language	● Teaching (9) ......*Reading*......	● Teaching (10) ......*Writing*......

 For further practice, do the Supplementary activity on page 110.

EXTRACT 3

| IELTS Listening Section 4 | Table/flow chart completion and multiple choice |

Questions 1–3

Complete the table below using **NO MORE THAN THREE WORDS** in each space.

Animal	Brought by	Reason
(1) Rabbit	settlers	for food
fox	settlers	(2) sport
cane toad	(3) sugar cane farmers	to kill beetles

Questions 4–5

Complete the flow chart using **NO MORE THAN THREE WORDS** in each space.

Beetle lays eggs.

Eggs become grubs.

Grubs eat (4) root .

Sugar cane (5) dies .

Questions 6–10

Circle the appropriate letter.

6 The cane toad originated in
   A Central America.
   B Hawaii.
   C Australia.

7 In Australia, the toads
   A grew extremely large.
   B multiplied in number.
   C ate the cane beetles.

8 The farmers' plan failed because
   A there were too many beetles.
   B their own research was faulty.
   C they believed reports they read.

9 The sugar cane industry
   A thrives today.
   B has died out in some areas.
   C survives alongside the beetle.

10 The second lesson to be learned from this story is that
   A the environment is constantly at risk.
   B first-hand research is not always necessary.
   C caution is necessary when dealing with nature.

The Reading Module

GENERAL READING STRATEGIES

When you go to university or college you may be overwhelmed by the amount of reading you are expected to do. You will have to do a lot of this reading on your own and you will need to be able to read *discriminatingly*. This means you will have to be selective about what you read. You will need to have the skills required to *focus in* on the information that is important to you and to *skim through* the information that isn't.

READING FOR IELTS

The IELTS examination tests your ability to read between 1500 and 2500 words in a fairly short period of time in order to find out certain information. In both the Academic and the General Training modules, you are given 60 minutes to answer a total of 40 questions. The texts and items are graded in terms of difficulty. If you can identify the reading skills being tested in each set of questions, and if you have some mastery of these skills, you will have a better chance of completing the Reading test successfully.

Academic Reading Module

The test has three reading passages and each of the passages is accompanied by a set of questions. There may be more than one type of question in each set. For example, you may be asked to find detailed information in a text in order to complete sentences; you may have to identify views and attitudes within a text; you may have to understand how something works and complete a diagram or chart. The passages may be written in a variety of different styles, such as argumentative, descriptive, narrative, discursive, etc.

General Training Reading Module

The test has three sections. Section 1 contains two or more texts which are based on social situations. Section 2 contains two texts based on course-related situations and Section 3 contains one text that tests general reading comprehension. The question types are similar to those in the Academic module. The texts in the first two sections are most likely to be descriptive and factual. The text in the third section may contain some argument.

If you are studying for the General Training modules you should begin with Reading Units 8 and 9.

Reading

In the IELTS test you are given texts to read which someone else has chosen for you. So it is important to skim through each text asking yourself the sort of questions that will help you understand it quickly.

- Re-read the introduction to the Reading module on the previous page and answer the following questions:

1 What subject is the text about?

2 Why was the text written?

3 Who was it written for?

4 Why would somebody read this text?

5 What type of text is it?

These are critical questions that help you to *orientate* yourself to the text.

TITLES AND SUB-HEADINGS

Nearly all articles that you read in magazines and newspapers will have a title (unless it has been removed for a particular reason). Many will also have a sub-heading.

- Read this title and sub-heading which introduce a magazine article:

The Dynamic Continent

The constantly changing landscape of Antarctica is a challenge to cartographers.*

Adrian Fox and Janet Thomson report.

*people who make maps

6 What is this article about?

7 What kind of person would be interested in this article?

8 What do you expect to read about in the first paragraph?

- Now read the first paragraph of the article:

IN MOST AREAS OF THE WORLD, certainly in Europe, both the physical landscape and the maps of it are relatively stable. Map revision is usually concerned with manmade features, such as buildings and roads. This is not true of Antarctica. The Antarctic ice sheet is a dynamic entity and cartographers have to contend with big and rapid changes in the physical geography of the continent. For example, earlier this year they faced the dramatic break-up of the Larsen and Prince Gustav ice shelves in the Antarctic Peninsula region, which is where the British Antarctic Survey (BAS) concentrates its mapping activity. Topographic maps are probably changing faster in Antarctica than anywhere else in the world.

• How useful were the title and the sub-heading in orientating you towards the text?

9 What is the writers' purpose in the first paragraph?

10 Is there a sentence that best summarises the main idea in this first paragraph?

These are the types of questions that you can ask yourself when you first read a text. They form part of our reading strategies.

• Read this title and sub-heading and discuss Questions 6–8 above with a partner:

WHY WE MUST BE STEWARDS* OF OUR SOIL

Managing this neglected resource is vital to our future, says John Houghton

*a person who manages something (like a park or property)

• Now read the first two paragraphs of the article:

Soil, air and water are the three essentials for life on land. But environmental policies have often taken soil for granted. Soil is of vital importance because we use it to produce our food. It is also an integral part of the landscapes and habitats we value so highly in the countryside.

We published our report, *Sustainable Use of Soil*, this week. In it, the Royal Commission on Environmental Pollution set out to establish what the effects would be if current human activities that affect soils, and present trends, continued unchanged for the next 100 years.

11 What do you learn about the writer and his purpose in the second paragraph?

12 How do you expect the article to continue?

13 How do you think the style of this article may be different from 'The Dynamic Continent'?

It is important to gradually build on your understanding of the information that is provided in each paragraph of a text. If you begin your reading by asking the type of questions you have met in this unit, you will begin to interact with the text immediately and you will be off to a good start.

 For more practice in reading titles and sub-headings, do Exercise A in the Supplementary activities on page 111.

PARAGRAPHS

As you read through each paragraph of an article, you gradually build on your understanding of what the writer is trying to say.

14 How does paragraphing help you do this?

15 When you first read a text, what should you look for in each paragraph?

- Read the title and sub-heading of the following article and discuss the content.
- Then go on to read the whole article.

The Undersea World of Sound

Snorts, clicks, whistles, groans – tune in to the long-distance language of the ocean

The vast oceans of the world are dark, deep and mysterious places where eyesight counts for little as soon as you venture very far beneath the surface.

For humans, who live in a world dominated by visual stimuli, to exist in such conditions would be impossible. But for whales and dolphins that live in the ocean or, in the case of a few species, muddy rivers and estuaries, the darkness is unimportant. What is crucial to them is sound.

Sound is an efficient way to transmit and sense information, especially as it travels five times faster through water than through air. If humans shout to someone, it is unlikely that they will be heard a kilometre away. But if a whale 'shouts' in an ocean channel, another whale may hear it tens, if not hundreds of kilometres away.

Whales and dolphins use sound in two ways: for communication and for echolocation. Dolphins, porpoises and toothed whales communicate through a wide variety of high-frequency sounds – pure tone whistles, pulsed squeals, screams or barks – generally at frequencies of 500Hz to 20kHz (where a hertz is a cycle per second and a kilohertz a thousand).

But as well as using sounds to communicate, toothed whales and dolphins also rely on echolocation to learn about their immediate environment, including prey that might be lurking nearby. They produce intense short broad-band pulses of sound in the ultrasonic range of between 0.25 and 220 kHz. These clicks are brief – typically less than one millisecond long – but they are repeated many times each second.

31

- Using a pencil, underline what you think is the key idea in each paragraph.
- Write a short paragraph that summarises the article.

16 What is the writer trying to do in the article?

    A explain the function of whale and dolphin sounds

    B account for the development of underwater sounds

    C compare the sounds made by whales and dolphins

    D give the results of his studies on underwater sounds

- Read the following opening to an article:

> THE DOMINANT FORMS of fictional narrative in our culture are the novel, the stage play and the motion picture (including television drama). I have had some experience of all three. I have been writing prose fiction for more than 30 years and think of myself primarily as a novelist. But some years ago I wrote a stage play which has had three professional productions; and over the same period I have adapted novels for television. Drawing upon that experience I want to explore what makes a writer tend towards one narrative medium rather than another, and what draws people to cross over from one to another.

17 An appropriate title for this paragraph would be

    A My life as a novelist

    B The difficulties of adaptation

    C Examining the choices writers make

    D A cultural perspective on entertainment

 Now do Exercise B in the Supplementary activities on page 111.

32

Reading

If you are asked to find a particular detail or piece of information in an IELTS passage, you will need to *skim* through the text fairly quickly, *scanning* for clues as to where the information might be found. This means you will need to read *faster than your normal pace*. There are a variety of IELTS question types that test your ability to extract specific information or details from a text. In nearly all cases, the information required is factual.

SHORT-ANSWER QUESTIONS

In this type of task, the questions test your ability to locate the right information in an article or passage. When you meet a set of short-answer questions in IELTS, you should read them carefully, before you go back to the text. In this way, you will know what you are looking for.

- Read through the following set of questions which are based on an article about sand. Underline the key words in each question.

1 What TWO substances made by humans are mentioned in the text?

2 Which part of a grain of sand have scientists measured?

3 What TWO factors determine the shape of a piece of sand?

4 How was the beach on Kamoama Island created?

5 Where, according to the text, can fine sandy beaches be found?

6 Who argues that sand is more efficient than coastal technology?

- Discuss what you have underlined in class.

7 Which answer do you think will be quickest to find in the text? Why?

8 Which answer(s) do you think will be hardest to locate in the text? Why?

- Read the article on the following page and underline the answers to Questions 1–6. Do this in ten minutes if you can.

TEST TIP

In a block of short-answer questions you will find that the answers occur in the text in the same order as the questions; i.e. you will come across the answer to question 1 first, and so on. Remember that when you move on to another block of questions you may have to start reading from the beginning of the text again.

Sifting through the Sands of Time

When you're on the beach, you're stepping on ancient mountains, skeletons of marine animals, even tiny diamonds. Sand provides a mineral treasure-trove, a record of geology's earth-changing processes

Sand: as children we play on it and as adults we relax on it. It is something we complain about when it gets in our food, and praise when it's moulded into castles. But we don't often look at it. If we did, we would discover an account of a geological past and a history of marine life that goes back thousands and in some cases millions of years.

Sand covers not just sea-shores, but also ocean beds, deserts and mountains. It is one of the most common substances on earth. And it is a major element in man-made materials too – concrete is largely sand, while glass is made of little else.

What exactly is sand? Well, it is larger than fine dust and smaller than shingle. In fact, according to the most generally accepted scheme of measurement, devised by the Massachusetts Institute of Technology, grains qualify if their diameter is greater than 0.06 of a millimetre and less than 0.6 of a millimetre.

Depending on its age and origin, a particular sand can consist of tiny pebbles or porous granules. Its grains may have the shape of stars or spirals, their edges jagged or smooth. They have come from the erosion of rocks, or from the skeletons of marine organisms, which accumulate on the bottom of the oceans, or even from volcanic eruptions.

Colour is another clue to sand's origins. If it is a dazzling white, its grains may be derived from nearby coral outcrops, from crystalline quartz rocks or from gypsum, like the white sands of New Mexico. On Pacific Islands jet black sands form from volcanic minerals. Other black beaches are magnetic. Some sand is very recent indeed, as is the case on the island of Kamoama in Hawaii, where a beach was created after a volcanic eruption in 1990. Molten lava spilled into the sea and exploded in glassy droplets.

Usually, the older the granules, the finer they are and the smoother their edges. The fine, white beaches of northern Scotland, for instance, are recycled from sandstone several hundred million years old. Perhaps they will be stone once more, in another few hundred million.

Sand is an irreplaceable industrial ingredient whose uses are legion: but it has one vital function you might never even notice. Sand cushions our land from the sea's impact, and geologists say it often does a better job of protecting our shores than the most advanced coastal technology.

TEST TIP
If you only give one answer when you are asked to give two you will be penalised.

- Discuss your answers to the six questions as a class. What sort of answers would lose marks?
- What other factual information could be tested in this passage?

LABELLING A DIAGRAM

This type of task often makes scanning easier because the information is located in *one* area of the text.

- Read the task and look at the diagram of the lighthouse on the next page.
- Scan the following article and circle the area of text that describes the lighthouse.

Divers hunt for ruins of Pharos lighthouse

Underwater archaeologists search the waters for Egyptian relics, Christopher Walker writes

A team of 30 divers is hurriedly searching the Mediterranean for the remains of the mighty Pharos lighthouse, built more than 2,200 years ago and regarded as one of the Seven Wonders of the ancient world.

In addition to Pharos, the joint French and Egyptian expedition is searching for the remnants of Greek temples and statues. The aim of the £300,000 project is to map a 23,920 sq yard area off Egypt's second largest city, founded by Alexander the Great. Under the water is a vast collection of ruins, some of which the 20 French and ten Egyptian divers hope to excavate and salvage. The team is hoping that among the remnants may be the lighthouse, built in 279 BC during the reign of Ptolemy II.

The huge white marble building was the marvel of its day. It was more than 400ft high in a colonnaded court and was equipped with a hydraulic lift to raise fuel to the roof. Its lantern, probably magnified by a reflecting device, could be seen over a radius of 34 miles. Within its square base were up to 300 rooms designed to house mechanics and operators; above were an octagonal storey and a circular storey, topped by a lantern with a beacon, the exact workings of which are still a mystery.

Although the lantern collapsed as early as the eighth century, the lighthouse served for 1,400 years as the symbol of Alexandria and a beacon for ships, until devastating earthquakes in 1100 and 1307 brought it tumbling down, presumably sending much of the debris into the sea surrounding Pharos island on which it was built.

The divers have made some fascinating discoveries, including at least three layers of blocks, some estimated to be as heavy as 70 tonnes, which may have been part of the lighthouse. "It is certainly possible that some of the pieces come from the lighthouse itself," said Jean-Pierre Cortegiani, a member of the expedition. "In fact, it would be amazing if nothing came from the lighthouse, seeing as this is where it toppled into the sea." Also discovered were hundreds of smaller blocks, thought to be pieces of temples and statues dating back to the Ptolemaic period. Among them were pieces of ancient columns, many inscribed, and huge granite and marble statues of sphinxes and Egyptian Gods, some of which stood 15ft high.

"We are making an identification of the blocks, studying the inscriptions and choosing some to be taken out," Cortegiani said. "We cannot take all the blocks out, but maybe we can have something like an underwater archaeological park."

- Complete the following IELTS task in ten minutes.

TEST TIP

In IELTS you will always be instructed to answer questions using NO MORE THAN THREE WORDS. This is important as you cannot fit many words onto the answer sheet.

IELTS Reading

Questions 9–13

*Label the diagram below which shows the parts of the lighthouse. Use **NO MORE THAN THREE WORDS** for each answer.*

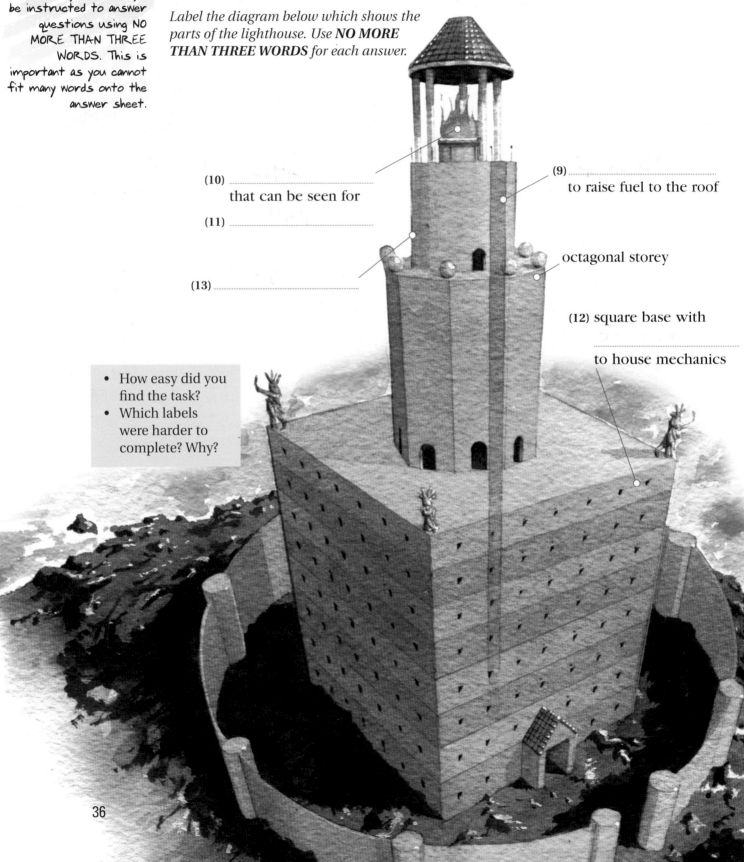

(10) ....
    that can be seen for

(11) ....

(13) ....

(9) ....
    to raise fuel to the roof

octagonal storey

(12) square base with
....
to house mechanics

- How easy did you find the task?
- Which labels were harder to complete? Why?

36

CHART/TABLE COMPLETION

IELTS Reading

Read the text below and answer Questions 14–19.

Baby Love

Why we want to take care of teddy bears

At the turn of the century, the first teddy bears had low foreheads, long snouts and long limbs like real bears. But over time, they have developed more baby-like features.

A group of scientists was curious to know whether teddies evolved this way because children demand baby-faced bears or because adults did. They gathered together eight pairs of teddies, each comprising a baby-faced bear and an adult-featured one. These teddies were shown to children aged four, six and eight years old.

When asked to choose their favourite bear from each pair, the older children (43 out of 54) preferred the baby-faced teddies. But the four-year-olds chose the baby-faced and adult-featured bears of each pair equally. When asked which one of all the bears they liked best, the older children chose more baby-faced bears but the four-year-olds preferred ones with adult features.

The scientists also asked the children what they would like to do with their favourite bear. The four-year-olds wanted to play with it, but the older children said they would like to sleep with the bear. The scientists suggest that young children do not develop a specific desire to look after the young and helpless until they are older.

Questions 14–19

*Complete the table below which shows the final results of the scientists' research. For Questions 14–17 use a tick (✓) for preference or cross (✗) for non-preference. For Questions 18–19 use **NO MORE THAN THREE WORDS**.*

Age of children	Baby-faced bears	Adult-featured bears	What they wanted to to do with bears
4 years	... (14) ✗	... (15) ...✓	... (18) ...play
8 years	... (16) ...✓	... (17) ...✗	... (19) ...sleep

 For further practice, do the Supplementary activity on page 111.

Reading

Most paragraphs in well-written discursive or argumentative texts contain at least one main idea and very often these ideas are supported by examples or by further explanation. IELTS tests your ability to identify main and supporting points and also to differentiate between them.

MULTIPLE CHOICE

- The following paragraph also occurs in Reading Unit 1, and is taken from an article on cartography (or map making). Read it and underline the main idea and any supporting points. Do this in five minutes.

> *In most areas of the world, certainly in Europe, both the physical landscape and the maps of it are relatively stable.* Map revision is usually concerned with manmade features, such as buildings and roads. This is not true of Antarctica. The Antarctic ice sheet is a dynamic entity and cartographers have to contend with big and rapid changes in the physical geography of the continent. For example, earlier this year they faced the dramatic break-up of the Larsen and Prince Gustav ice shelves in the Antarctic Peninsula region, which is where the British Antarctic Survey (BAS) concentrates its mapping activity. Topographic maps are probably changing faster in Antarctica than anywhere else in the world.

- Now do the multiple-choice question below.

1 What do the break-up of the Larsen and Prince Gustav ice shelves illustrate?
   A The errors that occur on maps of the Antarctic. ✗
   B The difficulties in reaching areas in the Antarctic. ✗
   C The sort of changes that can occur in the Antarctic.
   D The regularity with which map-makers visit the Antarctic.

2 What are the key words in each of the options A–D?

- Now read the following text. Underline the main ideas and note the number of supporting points. Do this in ten minutes.

GOING DIGITAL

Electronic libraries will make today's Internet pale by comparison. But building them will not be easy.

All over the world, libraries have begun the Herculean task of making faithful digital copies of the books, images and recordings that preserve the intellectual effort of humankind. For armchair scholars, the work promises to bring such a wealth of information to the desktop that the present Internet may seem amateurish in retrospect. ...

Librarians see three clear benefits to going digital. First, it helps them preserve rare and fragile objects without denying access to those who wish to study them. The British Library, for example, holds the only medieval manuscript of *Beowulf* in London. Only qualified scholars were allowed to see it until Kevin S. Kiernan of the University of Kentucky scanned the manuscript with three different light sources (revealing details not normally apparent to the naked eye) and put the images up on the Internet for anyone to peruse. Tokyo's National Diet Library is similarly creating highly detailed digital photographs of 1,236 woodblock prints, scrolls and other materials it considers national treasures so that researchers can scrutinise them without handling the originals.

A second benefit is convenience. Once books are converted to digital form, patrons can retrieve them in seconds rather than minutes. Several people can simultaneously read the same book or view the same picture. Clerks are spared the chore of reshelving. And libraries could conceivably use the Internet to lend their virtual collections to those who are unable to visit in person.

The third advantage of electronic copies is that they occupy millimeters of space on a magnetic disk rather than meters on a shelf. Expanding library buildings is increasingly costly. The University of California at Berkeley recently spent $46 million on an underground addition to house 1.5 million books – an average cost of $30 per volume. The price of disk storage, in contrast, has fallen to about $2 per 300-page publication and continues to drop.

3 What is the message in the first paragraph?

4 Which paragraphs in the text offer further explanation of the message?

5 Which words in the second paragraph help you identify the supporting points?

6 How easy would it be to write a summary of the text? Why?

Sometimes multiple-choice questions in IELTS have more than four options and you have to pick more than one correct answer. Look at the following question, which is based on the text above.

IELTS Reading

Questions 7–9

Which **THREE** *of the following are mentioned in the text as benefits of going digital?*

A More people can see precious documents. ✓
B Old manuscripts can be moved more easily.
C Material can be examined without being touched. ✓
D Fewer staff will be required in libraries.
E Borrowers need not go to the library building. ✓
F Libraries will be able to move underground. ✗

In this task you not only have to identify the benefits of libraries going digital, you also have to understand the wording in the question. Here the benefits are expressed in a different way and this is called *paraphrasing*.

- Look carefully at how the original meaning has been paraphrased in A–F.
- Discuss why the other options are wrong.
- Underline and paraphrase some of the other benefits mentioned in the text.
- Write a summary of the text for homework.

NOTE-TAKING

Taking notes from written sources is one of the main skills you will need when you go to university. Typically, note-taking involves the reader in identifying the main and supporting points in a text.

- Read the following newspaper article and see if you can locate any main and supporting ideas. Make a note of these.

'Salty' rice plant boosts harvests

British scientists are breeding a new generation of rice plants that will be able to grow in soil contaminated with salt water. Their work may enable abandoned farms to become productive once more, *writes Sean Hargrave*.

Tim Flowers and Tony Yeo, from Sussex University's School of Biological Sciences, have spent several years researching how crops, such as rice, could be made to grow in water that has become salty.

The pair have recently begun a three-year programme, funded by the Biotechnology and Biological Sciences Research Council, to establish which genes enable some plants to survive saline conditions. The aim is to breed this capability into crops, starting with rice.

It is estimated that each year more than 10m hectares of agricultural land are lost because salt gets into the soil and stunts plants. The problem is caused by

several factors. In the tropics, mangroves that create swamps and traditionally form barriers to sea water have been cut down. In the Mediterranean, a series of droughts have caused the water table to drop, allowing sea water to seep in. In Latin America, irrigation often causes problems when water is evaporated by the heat, leaving salt deposits behind.

Excess salt then enters the plants and prevents them functioning normally. Heavy concentrations of minerals in the plants curb the process of osmosis and stop them drawing up the water they need to survive.

To overcome these problems, Flowers and Yeo decided to breed rice plants that take in very little salt and store what they do absorb in cells that do not affect the plant's growth. They have started to breed these characteristics into a new rice crop, but it will take about eight

harvests until the resulting seeds are ready to be considered for commercial use.

Once the characteristics for surviving salty soil are known, Flowers and Yeo will try to breed the appropriate genes into all manner of crops and plants. Land that has been abandoned to nature will then be able to bloom again, providing much needed food in the poorer countries of the world.

- Now look at the notes in the IELTS activity on the next page.

IELTS Reading

Questions 10–13

*Complete the notes below. Choose **ONE** OR **TWO WORDS** from the passage for each answer. Write your answers in boxes 10–13 on your answer sheet.*

Aim of research: to identify … **(10)** … that promote growth in salt water
                     genes

Problem: salt inhibits plant growth

Causes of problem:

* natural … **(11)** … to sea water have been destroyed   *(in tropics)*
   barriers
* water levels have gone down after … **(12)** … *(in Mediterranean)*
   droughts
* salt remains after … **(13)** … *(in Latin America)*
   water evaporates / irrigation

 For further IELTS practice, do the Supplementary activity on page 111.

TEST TIP

You will be expected to complete the notes using words that are printed in the passage when the instructions state that this is required. If you do not do this and you use words that are not given in the passage, you may be penalised.

Reading

Writers make use of paragraphing to divide a text into manageable sections for the reader. A new paragraph usually introduces a new point, theme or angle to the text and as a reader you should be able to recognise what this is. Making a mental note of the main idea(s) in each paragraph is an important reading skill. IELTS tests you on your ability to do this through paragraph heading tasks.

PARAGRAPH HEADINGS

- Some texts, particularly newspaper articles or reports, have headings so that the reader can quickly skim through and get a good idea of the content. The following newspaper article has five paragraphs (A–E) but the headings have been removed. Read it and write your own title for each of the paragraphs. Do this in 20 minutes.

Succeeding in title role

Magazine circulations are in the millions and advertising revenue is rising despite the growth of TV and electronic media, reports David Short

A Print is not dead yet – at least not when it comes to magazines. Despite ever-growing competition from television and electronic media, a new report shows that worldwide advertising expenditure in consumer magazines has doubled over the past decade.

B The report also shows that many magazines in Europe continue to enjoy circulations in the millions, despite the ever-growing number of television channels, whether cable, satellite, terrestrial, analogue, or digital, and the incursion of the Internet. And new French research has revealed that magazines are still powerful tools for owners of brands.

C Advertising expenditure worldwide was $225 billion last year, according to the report *World Magazine Trends*. $32 billion of this, or 14%, was taken by magazines. In Europe, the share of consumer magazine advertising expenditure was $12 billion or 21% of an estimated overall spend of $57 billion. But the share has dropped in the past 15 years from 30 per cent, with decline having been particularly severe in Belgium and Germany where commercial television was introduced relatively late.

D However, the types of magazines which Europeans choose to flip through still varies dramatically according to country, with few signs that the European magazine with a common title is making inroads across nations. Interests which can create top-selling titles in one country are nowhere to be seen in the circulation lists of others.

E But whatever their relative importance across Europe, magazines have one real advantage over broadcast media. For advertisers such as tobacco and alcohol producers, which are barred or severely restricted on television in some countries, magazines remain a safe haven for their messages.

Follow-up

- Compare your heading for each paragraph with the headings that other students in your class have written.
- Discuss the main ideas in each paragraph and decide if some headings are better than others.
- Were any of the paragraphs more difficult to write headings for? Why?
- Look back at your headings. Where you didn't use your own words, try doing so now.

 For further practice, do Exercise A in the Supplementary activities on page 112.

The IELTS Reading component often tests candidates on their ability to select a heading for each paragraph in a text, from a list of headings.

IELTS Reading

How to approach the task

- ► Take 10 minutes to read the passage on the following pages, underlining what you think are the *main ideas* and *key vocabulary* in each paragraph.
- ► Read through the list of headings to familiarise yourself with them.
- ► Look carefully at the example – in this case, paragraph A.
- ► Re-read paragraph B and select the heading that best fits this paragraph. Continue this procedure with paragraphs C–H. Take about 15 minutes to do this.

Questions 1–7

The Reading Passage on the following pages has eight paragraphs (A–H). Choose the most suitable heading for each paragraph from the list of headings below. Write the appropriate numbers (i–x) in boxes 1–7 on your answer sheet.

NB *There are more headings than paragraphs so you will not use all of them.*
   You may use any heading more than once.

List of Headings

✓i	Benefiting from an earlier model
✓ii	Important operative conditions
iii	Examining the public confusion
iv	Where to go from here?
✓v	How it's all linked up
✓vi	Finding a suitable location
vii	Comparing wind speeds in Australian cities
✓viii	Matching operational requirements with considerations of appearance
✓ix	What makes Esperance different?
x	What is a wind farm?

TEST TIP

You will always get an example paragraph in IELTS but it may not be the first paragraph.

Example	Answer
Paragraph A	x

1 Paragraph B   4 Paragraph E   7 Paragraph H

2 Paragraph C   5 Paragraph F

3 Paragraph D   6 Paragraph G

AUSTRALIA'S FIRST COMMERCIAL WIND FARM

It's two years since the rotor blades began spinning in Esperance, Western Australia

A HARVEST time in Esperance is constant. As long as the wind blows – which is pretty much all the time – nine identical synchronised wind turbines reap the benefits of the dependable winds that gust up around the southern coastline of Western Australia. These sleek, white, robot-like wind turbines loom up on the horizon forming part of Australia's first commercial wind farm. They're not only functional machines that help provide electricity for this secluded coastal town, but increasingly, they're also drawcards for curious tourists and scientists alike.

B Because of its isolation, Esperance is not linked to Western Power's grid which supplies electricity from gas-, coal- and oil-fired power stations to the widespread population of Western Australia. Before the wind turbines went in, Esperance's entire electricity needs were met by the diesel power station in town.

C The $5.8 million Ten Mile Lagoon project is not Esperance's first wind farm. The success of a smaller, experimental wind farm, at a spot called Salmon Beach, encouraged the State's power utility to take Esperance wind seriously. Today, the wind turbines at Ten Mile Lagoon work in conjunction with the diesel power station, significantly reducing the amount of the town's electricity generated by expensive diesel power.

D   The wind farm is connected to the power station by a 33-kilovolt powerline, and a radio link between the two allows operators to monitor and control each wind turbine. The nine 225-kilowatt Vestas wind turbines produce a total generating capacity of two megawatts and provide around 12 per cent of the energy requirements of Esperance and its surrounding districts.

E   The power produced by a wind turbine depends on the size and efficiency of the machine and, of course, on the energy in the wind. The energy in the wind available to the wind turbines is proportional to wind speed cubed. Thus, the greater the wind speed, the greater the output of the turbine. In order to achieve optimum wind speeds, the right location is imperative. "You have to accept the nature of the beast," Mr Rosser, Western Power's physicist said. "As surface dwellers our perceptions of wind speeds are bad. As you go higher, wind speed increases significantly."

F   The most favourable wind sites are on gently sloping hills, away from obstructions like trees and buildings and where the prevailing winds are not blocked. Computer modelling was used to select the best site for Esperance's wind farm. Scientists were concerned not only with efficiency, but also with protecting the coastal health environment which is rich in plant life and home to tiny pygmy and honey-possums, and a host of bird species. In addition, the wind farm is adjacent to Esperance's popular scenic tourist drive.

G   Strict erosion controls have been implemented and access to the wind farm is limited to selected viewing areas. The wind turbine towers are painted white and devoid of corporate logos or signage. According to Mr Rosser there is something of a worldwide backlash against wind farms with regard to their visual impact. "But because wind turbines perform best in the most exposed positions, they will always be visible. There is a very real need to balance environmental and technical requirements. I think the Ten Mile Lagoon Wind Farm sets the standards for environmentally friendly developments."

H   In fact, the project has become something of a tourist attraction in itself. Esperance shire president Ian Mickel said the wind turbines had been well accepted by locals. "We have watched the wind farm develop with great interest, and now we find visitors to Esperance are equally enthusiastic about it," he said. The aim now is to identify other remote locations where wind turbines will be a feasible means of supplementing existing power stations.

8 What is the writer doing in the article?

  A responding to criticism of a project

  B reviewing the success of a project ✓

  C explaining his role in a project

  D predicting the future of a project

 Now do Exercise B in the Supplementary activities on page 112.

Reading

A question that may be used in IELTS to test your understanding of the main ideas in a passage is a summary with gaps and a box of possible answers to choose from. The summary may cover the main ideas presented over a large area of the text and so it will be necessary for you to have a good understanding of these. In addition, the summary will *paraphrase* the points in the text so you will need to be familiar with different ways of expressing the same idea.

COMPLETING A SUMMARY

When we read, we tend to make a mental note of the main ideas of a text so that we have an overall understanding of it. Use your global reading skills to familiarise yourself with the following passage.

Prehistoric insects spawn new drugs

by Steve Connor, Science Correspondent

A   Insects entombed in fossilised amber for tens of millions of years have provided the key to creating a new generation of antibiotic drugs that could wage war on modern diseases. Scientists have isolated the antibiotics from microbes found either inside the intestines of the amber-encased insects or in soil particles trapped with them when they were caught by sticky tree resin up to 130 million years ago. Spores of the microbes have survived an unprecedented period of suspended animation, enabling scientists to revive them in the laboratory.

B   Research over the past two years has uncovered at least four antibiotics from the microbes and one has been able to kill modern drug-resistant bacteria that can cause potentially deadly diseases in humans. Present-day antibiotics have nearly all been isolated from micro-organisms that use them as a form of defence against their predators or competitors. But since the introduction of antibiotics into medicine 50 years ago, an alarming number have become ineffective because many bacteria have developed resistance to the drugs. The antibiotics that were in use millions of years ago may prove more deadly against drug-resistant modern strains of disease-causing bacteria.

C   Raul Cano, who has pioneered the research at the

California Polytechnic State University at San Luis Obispo, said the ancient antibiotics had been successful in fighting drug-resistant strains of staphylococcus bacteria, a "superbug" that has threatened the health of patients in hospitals throughout the world. He now intends to establish whether the antibiotics might have harmful side effects. "The problem is how toxic it is to other cells and how easy it is to purify," said Cano.

D A biotechnology company, Ambergene, has been set up to develop the antibiotics into drugs. If any ancient microbes are revived that resemble present-day diseases, they will be destroyed in case they escape and cause new epidemics. Drug companies will be anxious to study the chemical structures of the prehistoric antibiotics to see how they differ from modern drugs. They hope that one ancient antibiotic molecule could be used as a basis to synthesise a range of drugs.

E There have been several attempts to extract material such as DNA from fossilised life-forms ranging from Egyptian mummies to dinosaurs but many were subsequently shown to be contaminated. Cano's findings have been hailed as a break-through by scientists. Edward Golenberg, an expert on extracting DNA from fossilised life-forms at Wayne State University in Detroit, said: "They appear to be verifiable, ancient spores. They do seem to be real." Richard Lenski, professor of microbial ecology at Michigan State University, said the fight against antibiotic-resistant strains of bacteria, such as tuberculosis and staphylococcus, could be helped by the discovery.

F However, even the discovery of ancient antibiotics may not halt the rise of drug-resistant bacteria. Stuart Levy, a micro-biologist at Tufts University in Boston, warned that the bacteria would eventually evolve to fight back against the new drugs. "There might also be an enzyme already out there that can degrade it. So the only way to keep the life of that antibiotic going is to use it sensibly and not excessively," he said.

- Skim through the passage again and underline the main ideas in each paragraph.
- Write a sentence that summarises each paragraph.

Follow-up

- When you have finished, compare your sentences with those of your partner. Discuss which sentences capture the main ideas best.
- Write a sub-heading for the article and discuss the writer's purpose and intended readers.

UNDERSTANDING PARAPHRASE

- On the following page is a summary of the main ideas in the article you have just read, but to make it easier, it has been broken down into gapped sentences.
- See if you can complete the sentences by selecting the correct word from the box below the summary.

SUMMARY

Microbes that may supply new antibiotic drugs, have been ... **(1)** ... in the bodies of fossilised insects.

The discovery may help destroy bacteria that are no longer ... **(2)** ... to modern medicine.

What needs to be done now is to find out how ... **(3)** ... the antibiotics will be.

Microbes that seem to have the characteristics of ... **(4)** ... diseases will have to be killed.

It is thought that a ... **(5)** ... molecule could lead to a whole series of drugs.

Other scientists who have tried to produce antibiotics in a similar way have been ... **(6)** ...

This work is considered a ... **(7)** ... achievement.

It is necessary to be ... **(8)** ... about maintaining the life of the antibiotics.

LIST OF WORDS

deadly	resistant	responding	modern
safe	significant	preserved	single
unsuccessful	successful	careful	prehistoric
combined	particular	contributing	lifetime
unusual	placed	serious	excited

Follow-up

- Discuss with your teacher how much of the text was covered in each of the paraphrased points. Also examine the techniques that were used to summarise the ideas in the text.
- Which words were hardest to find? Why do you think this was?
- Link all the paraphrased points together to make a paragraph that summarises the text. (When you have done this, you will have a typical example of the types of summary paragraph you may meet in the IELTS test.)

 For further IELTS practice, do the Supplementary activity on page 112.

Reading

UNIT 6 Understanding argument

Some texts are completely factual, for example texts in an encyclopaedia, or factual reports or reviews. Many texts, however, contain some argument or opinion. At least one of the texts you will meet in the IELTS test will contain some detailed logical arguments and you will be tested on your ability to identify and understand these arguments as they are presented in the passage.

ARGUMENT OR FACT?

• Skim through the following passage and highlight those areas which deal with arguments and those that simply present facts.

Penguins show signs of stress

A new argument has been put forward as to whether penguins are disturbed by the presence of tourists in Antarctica.

Previous research by scientists from Keil University in Germany monitored Adelie penguins and noted that the birds' heart rates increased dramatically at the sight of a human as far as 30 metres away. But new research using an artificial egg, which is equipped to measure heart rates, disputes this. Scientists from the Scott Polar Research Institute at Cambridge say that a slow moving human who does not approach the nest too closely, is not perceived as a threat by penguins.

The earlier findings have been used to partly explain the 20 per cent drop in populations of certain types of penguins near tourist sites. However, tour operators have continued to insist that their activities do not adversely affect wildlife in Antarctica, saying they encourage non-disruptive behaviour in tourists, and that the decline in penguin numbers is caused by other factors.

Amanda Nimon of the Scott Polar Research Institute spent three southern hemisphere summers at Cuverville Island in Antarctica studying penguin behaviour towards humans. "A nesting penguin will react very differently to a person rapidly and closely approaching the nest," says Nimon. "First they exhibit large and prolonged heart rate changes and then they often flee the nest leaving it open for predators to fly in and remove eggs or chicks."

The artificial egg, specially developed for the project, monitored both the parent who had been 'disturbed' when the egg was placed in the nest and the other parent as they both took it in turns to guard the nest.

However, Boris Culik, who monitored the Adelie penguins, believes that Nimon's findings do not invalidate his own research. He points out that species behave differently – and Nimon's work was with Gentoo penguins. Nimon and her colleagues believe that Culik's research was methodologically flawed because the monitoring of penguins' responses entailed capturing and restraining the birds and fitting them with heart-rate transmitters. Therefore, argues Nimon, it would not be surprising if they became stressed on seeing a human subsequently.

1 Why do you think this article was written?

2 What do you notice about the views presented in it?

3 What overall message is presented?

4 What would be a suitable sub-heading for the article?

Now look at the following multiple-choice question. This is one way in which you may be tested on your ability to identify the arguments presented in a text.

IELTS Reading

How to approach the task

► Underline the key words in the arguments A–F.
► Then scan the text for expressions of the same idea.

Questions 5–7

*Which **THREE** of the following arguments are stated in the text?*

A Penguins are not afraid of people who behave calmly. ✓

B Penguins need better protection from tourists.

C Not all penguins behave in the same way. ✓

D Tourists are not responsible for the fall in penguin numbers. ✓

E Penguins are harder to research when they have young.

F Tour operators should encourage tourists to avoid Antarctica.

 For further practice in understanding and paraphrasing arguments, do the **Supplementary activity on page 113.**

MATCHING

Sometimes a matching exercise is used in IELTS to test your ability to identify and understand different arguments. It is used particularly when the text presents a number of arguments or theories from different sources.

• Read the following extract from an article on Australia's farming and highlight the different sources (people or organisations) quoted in the article.

• Select some of the arguments and see if you can paraphrase them.

Australia's Growing Disaster

Farming is threatening to destroy the soil and native flora and fauna over vast areas of Australia. What price should be put on conservation?

Australia's National Greenhouse Gas Inventory Committee estimates that burning wood from cleared forests accounts for about 30 per cent of Australia's emissions of carbon dioxide, or 156 million tonnes a year. And water tables are rising beneath cleared land. In the Western Australian wheat belt, estimates suggest that water is rising by up to 1 metre a year. The land is becoming waterlogged and unproductive or is being poisoned by salt, which is brought to the surface. The Australian Conservation Foundation (ACF) reckons that 33 million hectares has been degraded by salination. The federal government estimates the loss in production from salinity at A$200 million a year.

According to Jason Alexandra of the ACF, this list of woes is evidence that Australia is depleting its resources by trading agricultural commodities for manufactured imports. In effect, it sells topsoil for technologies that will be worn out or redundant in a few years. The country needs to get away from the "colonial mentality" of exploiting resources and adopt agricultural practices suited to Australian conditions, he says.

Robert Hadler of the National Farmers' Federation (NFF) does not deny that there is a problem, but says that it is "illogical" to blame farmers. Until the early 1980s, farmers were given tax incentives to clear land because that was what people wanted. If farmers are given tax breaks to manage the land sustainably, they will do so. Hadler argues that the two reports on land clearance do not say anything which was not known before.

Australia is still better off than many other developed countries, says Dean Graetz, an ecologist at the CSIRO, the national research organisation. "A lot of the country is still notionally pristine," he says. "It is not transformed like Europe where almost nothing that is left is natural." Graetz, who analysed the satellite photographs for the second land clearance report, argues that there is now better co-operation between Australian scientists, government officials and farmers than in the past.

But the vulnerable state of the land is now widely understood, and across Australia, schemes have started for promoting environment friendly farming. In 1989, Prime Minister Bob Hawke set up Landcare, a network of more than 2000 regional conservation groups. About 30 percent of landholders are members. "It has become a very significant social movement," says Helen Alexander from the National Landcare Council. "We started out worrying about not much more than erosion and the replanting of trees but it has grown much more diverse and sophisticated."

But the bugbear of all these conservation efforts is money. Landcare's budget is A$110 million a year, of which only A$6 million goes to farmers. Neil Clark, an agricultural consultant from Bendigo in Victoria, says that farmers are not getting enough. "Farmers may want to make more efficient use of water and nutrients and embrace more sustainable practices, but it all costs money and they just don't have the spare funds," he says.

Clark also says scientists are taking too large a share of the money for conservation. Many problems posed by agriculture to the environment have been "researched to death", he says. "We need to divert the money for a while into getting the solutions into place." Australia's chief scientist, Michael Pitman, disagrees. He says that science is increasingly important. Meteorologists, for example, are becoming confident about predicting events which cause droughts in Australia. "If this can be done with accuracy then it will have immense impact on stocking levels and how much feed to provide," says Pitman. "The end result will be much greater efficiency."

Steve Morton of the CSIRO Division of Wildlife and Ecology says the real challenge facing conservationists is to convince the 85 per cent of Australians who live in cities that they must foot a large part of the bill. "The land is being used to feed the majority and to produce wealth that circulates through the financial markets of the cities," he says. One way would be to offer incentives to extend the idea of stewardship to areas outside the rangelands, so that more land could be protected rather than exploited. Alexander agrees. "The nation will have to debate to what extent it is willing to support rural communities," she says. "It will have to decide to what extent it wants food prices to reflect the true cost of production. That includes the cost of looking after the environment."

- What is the writer's purpose in this article?
- How is the writer using the arguments?

IELTS Reading

How to approach the task

► The statements 8–15 below are simply paraphrases of the arguments presented in the text.

► Skim through the list of statements and the list of people once before you begin the task, just to get an impression of the views and people you will be looking for.

► Begin reading the passage and stop when you come to the first person's name and their view.

► Skim through the list of statements looking for one that matches. In the first instance this is Jason Alexandra (JA) and the view expressed in Question 12.

► Continue reading the passage until you come to the next person and view. In this way you may save yourself some time.

Questions 8–15

TEST TIP

Unlike the short-answer questions, these views are listed in random order; that is, they are not in the order in which they occur in the passage.

Match the views (8–15) with the people listed in the box below.

NB *You may have to use some people more than once.*

8   Current conservation schemes are taking many problems into account.

9   Ordinary people will have to help pay for conservation.

10 Conserving land is too expensive for farmers.

11 The Government can encourage farmers to do what it wants them to do.

12 Australia should review its import/export practices.

13 More conservation funds should be put into practical projects.

14 Much of the land in Australia is still unspoilt.

15 Research is necessary to help solve conservation problems.

People	
JA	Jason Alexandra
RH	Robert Hadler
DG	Dean Graetz
HA	Helen Alexander
NC	Neil Clark
MP	Michael Pitman
SM	Steve Morton

Reading

IELTS frequently tests candidates on their ability to identify opinions and views as they are presented in a text. The terms 'views' or 'claims' are used in the test instructions and may refer to arguments or opinions put forward by the writer or by other people referred to by the writer.

FACT, OPINION OR CLAIM?

1 Read the following excerpts from articles and decide whether they are giving an opinion, making a claim or presenting a fact.

a Like crying and laughing, yawning is a variation of normal breathing. It is a reflex action that is not under conscious control.

c Based on our findings, future changes to Antarctic maps resulting from major improvements in source information are likely to be minimal.

b I find playing a Shakespearean character very different from giving a concert or doing an emotional scene in a film. Performing music doesn't take that kind of concentration.

d Many companies have schemes that reward high sales but in my experience they fail to take notice of the 'backroom' members of the teams who help to make such sales possible.

e At the tender age of just three months, little boys can detect a difference between male and female babies – and it seems they like the boys better, say researchers in Britain.

• Read the article below and continue to highlight some of the facts and opinions in it.

Books, Films and Plays

The novelist's medium is the written word, one might almost say the printed word; the novel as we know it was born with the invention of printing. Typically, the novel is consumed by a silent, solitary reader, who may be anywhere at the time. The paperback novel is still the cheapest, most portable and adaptable form of narrative entertainment. It is limited to a single channel of information – writing. But within that restriction it is the most versatile of narrative forms. The narrative can go, effortlessly, anywhere: into space, people's heads, palaces, prisons and pyramids, without any consideration of cost or practical feasibility. In determining the shape and content of his narrative, the writer of prose fiction is constrained by nothing except purely artistic criteria.

This does not necessarily make his task any easier than that of the writer of plays and screenplays, who must always be conscious of practical constraints such as budgets, performance time, casting requirements, and so on. The very infinity of choice enjoyed by the novelist is a source of anxiety and difficulty. But the novelist does retain absolute control over his text until it is published and received by the audience. He may be advised by his editor to revise his text, but if the writer refused to meet this condition no one would be surprised. It is not unknown for a well established novelist to deliver his or her manuscript and expect the publisher to print it exactly as written. However, not even the most well established playwright or screenplay writer would submit a script and expect it to be performed without any rewriting. This is because plays and motion pictures are collaborative forms of narrative, using more than one channel of communication.

The production of a stage play involves, as well as the words of the author, the physical presence of the actors, their voices and gestures as orchestrated by the director, spectacle in the form of lighting and "the set", and possibly music. In film, the element of spectacle is more prominent in the sequence of visual images, heightened by various devices of perspective and focus. In film too, music tends to be more pervasive and potent than in straight drama. So, although the script is the essential basis of both stage play and film, it is a basis for subsequent revision negotiated between the writer and the other creative people involved; in the case of the screenplay, the writer may have little or no control over the final form of his work. Contracts for the production of plays protect the rights of authors in this respect. They are given "approval" of the choice of director and actors and have the right to attend rehearsals. Often a good deal of rewriting takes place in the rehearsal period and sometimes there is an opportunity for more rewriting during previews before the official opening night.

In film or television work, on the other hand, the screenplay writer usually has no contractual right to this degree of consultation. Practice in this respect varies very much from one production company to another, and according to the nature of the project and the individuals involved. In short, while the script is going through its various drafts, the writer is in the driver's seat, albeit receiving advice and criticism from the producer and the director. But once the production is under way, artistic control over the project tends to pass to the director. This is a fact overlooked by most journalistic critics of television drama, who tend (unlike film critics) to give all the credit or blame for success or failure of a production to the writer and actors, ignoring the contribution, for good or ill, of the director.

2 What type of article is this?

A a review
B a case study
C a narrative
D a discussion

YES, NO, NOT GIVEN

A task that is often used to test your understanding of the writer's message is one that provides a list of possible views or claims and asks you if they agree with what the writer says or not.

IELTS Reading

Do the following statements agree with the claims of the writer in the Reading Passage? Write:

YES	*if the statement agrees with the writer*
NO	*if the statement contradicts the writer*
NOT GIVEN	*if there is no information about this in the passage*

How to approach the task

► Take some time to read the rubric to this task carefully, so that you understand the difference between a 'NO' answer and a 'NOT GIVEN' answer. If you write 'NO' as your answer, you are saying that the claim expressed in the question is **the opposite of** the view presented in the passage. This is quite different from a 'NOT GIVEN' answer which says that you can find **nothing in the passage about this idea**.

► Read each statement carefully, noting the key words and making sure you understand what is meant by each of them.

► Then skim through the article to see if you can locate a similar or opposite idea.

► Look at the example. The key words are *novelists, concern, difficulties, other artists*. The statement is a paraphrase of the last sentence in the first paragraph and parts of the first sentence in the next paragraph.

► Now complete the exercise.

Example	*Answer*
Novelists do not have to concern themselves with many of the difficulties faced by other artists.	NOT GIVEN

Y **3** Novelists have fewer restrictions on their work than playwrights.

N **4** Novelists must agree to the demands of their editors.

NG **5** Playwrights envy the simplicity of the novelist's work.

N **6** Music is a more significant element of theatre than cinema.

NG **7** Experience in the theatre improves the work of screenplay writers.

Y **8** Playwrights can revise their work continuously.

Y **9** Directors usually have the final say in how a TV drama will turn out.

 For further IELTS practice, do the Supplementary activity on page 113.

TEST TIP

The YES and NO questions will be presented in the order in which the answers occur in the text.

IDENTIFYING ATTITUDE AND MAKING INFERENCES

It is difficult to identify attitudes and infer meaning because often you need to understand something that is not directly stated. For example, in the third paragraph of the text on the previous page, it is possible to infer (or deduce) that screenplay writers are sometimes barred from rehearsals, although this is not directly stated.

IELTS recognises that these are very demanding reading skills and so they are not tested very often. If they are tested, the common task-type is a multiple-choice question which offers a number of possible interpretations of a view/argument and requires you to select the correct one.

10 Read the following extracts from various articles and discuss what inferences you can make from them and whether you can identify the writer's attitude.

> **a** Dr Masson recounts tales of animal rescues, favours, longings, friendships and enmities. But he does himself no favours with his own emotive language, which will alienate many scientists. Animals are referred to throughout by the pronoun 'who' rather than 'which', for example.

> **c** The hardline view is that animals do not have the consciousness or self-awareness required for emotional feeling. This is a convenient assumption for a society that keeps animals in homes, zoos, farms and laboratories.

> **b** My grandmother had no redeeming features. She was huge and always directed all her hugeness at me when she came to stay with us. Her arms were strong enough to strangle a bear, let alone a five-year-old boy. I knew if I were to live to be a man, I would have to find some protection against my grandmother.

IELTS Reading

Read the following extract from a book review and answer Questions 11–13.

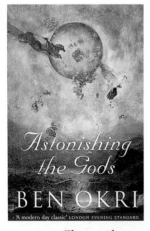

Astonishing the Gods by Ben Okri is not for the habitually cynical. Nor, even if you're not a habitual cynic, is it the kind of book that should be read on a day when the real world is likely to intrude. This book oozes escapism. But it isn't easy or simple to digest.

So, to avoid irritation, do not try to read this short but intense novel on your way to work or at times when you might have to stop to answer telephone calls or cope with domestic or other practicalities. Also, avoid it like the plague if you are hooked on straightforward linear narratives or if you're the sort of person who can only identify with trees that are trees and buildings that don't dissolve into thin air.

Apologies for appearing to labour this point about who should read Okri and about when and how he should be read. But he has been so harshly criticised by the impatiently earthbound that the point cannot be made strongly enough. If you aren't capable of – or in the mood for – locking yourself away for a few hours and allowing your mind to drift in a dreamlike state down magical, mythical avenues, you'd be best to settle for a book with a 'normal' plot, tangible landscapes and effortlessly understandable characters.

Choose the appropriate letters A–D and write them in boxes 11–13 on your answer sheet.

11 According to the writer, the book should be read
  A several times.
  B in short bursts.
  C with an open mind.
  D by an experienced reader.

12 The book contains
  A offensive material.
  B a complex story.
  C life-like characters.
  D imaginative humour.

13 Some readers have failed to
  A appreciate Okri's style.
  B understand Okri's message.
  C recognise the setting of the book.
  D finish reading the book.

Reading

How much do you know about the IELTS General Training (GT) Reading module? (Check your answers with the introductory section.)

1 How many sections are there?

2 How long do you have to answer the questions?

3 How many questions are there?

The GT Reading module presents a series of graded texts and accompanying questions that test a variety of reading skills. The task types are similar to those used in the Academic module and Section 3 of the GT module is the same as an Academic Reading section. However, the text types in GT Sections 1 and 2 are very different from those in the Academic module.

4 Approximately how long should you spend on Section 1?

5 What is the general theme of the texts in Section 1?

MULTIPLE CHOICE

In Section 1, you are most likely to be tested on your ability to find or identify factual information, but you may also have to use your skills to deduce or infer an answer. Texts in Section 1 of the General Training module are short and may take a variety of formats.

• Read the following advertisements and answer the multiple-choice questions.

6 This is an advertisement for

   A a pocket calculator.
   B binoculars.
   C a camera.
   D sunglasses.

CAVRON

Sureshot M

Ideal pocket autofocus compact, fully automatic, high quality lens

NOW ONLY
£89

was £129   VISA & MASTERCARD

7 What sort of event is being advertised?

   A a circus
   B a film
   C a fashion display
   D a talk

TRAVELS WITH A MEXICAN CIRCUS

Tuesday 13th September at 7.30 pm

Travel writer **Katie Hickman** recalls remote and beautiful parts of Mexico and its people, during the year she spent with a circus troupe.

TICKETS REQUIRED

TEST TIP

When you are being tested on advertisements, remember that a lot of information can be given in these and you should be careful to scan the texts as thoroughly as possible. At the same time, you should bear in mind that you do not need to understand everything in the texts to be able to answer the questions.

8 The price for this mosquito net includes

   A something to carry it in.
   B a tube of repellant.
   C an impregnation kit.
   D a treated pillow.

BOTHERED BY INSECTS?

Don't let mosquitoes ruin your holiday sleep or your health!

A lightweight (500g) mosquito net for travellers complete with spreader frame, supports and compact (80cm x 30cm) zippered bag. Pre-treated with a synthetic pyrethoid permethrin (as recommended by the World Health Organisation) adding repellency to the physical barrier.

Total cost delivered £29
Impregnation kits £6.50

APPROPRIATE APPLICATIONS
24 Hour Tel/Fax 01352 762936

9 The advertisement suggests that the net can

   A be used by children.
   B fold up to a small size.
   C be enlarged to fit any bed.
   D be zipped or sewn.

TRUE, FALSE, NOT GIVEN

This is another type of task that may be used to test your ability to scan for specific information.

IELTS Reading (GT)

How to approach the task

It is worth taking some time to read the rubric to this task carefully so that you understand the difference between a 'FALSE' answer and a 'NOT GIVEN' answer. If you write 'FALSE' as your answer, you are saying that the information expressed in the question is **the opposite of** that presented in the text. This is quite different from a 'NOT GIVEN' answer, which says that you can find **nothing in the text about this information**.

Read the advertisement below and answer Questions 10–13 by writing

TRUE   *if the statement is true*
FALSE   *if the statement is false*
NOT GIVEN   *if no information is given about this*

> ## CHESTFIELD CARS
>
> - AIRPORT SERVICES a speciality
> - Well established & reliable
> - Up to 4 persons
>
> **£35 to GATWICK AIRPORT**
> **£45 to HEATHROW AIRPORT**
>
> - No destination too far!
> - Discount for return bookings
> - 8-seater minibus available
>
> **(0227) 70 30 90**

10 It will cost £35 for two people to go to Gatwick. T

11 Chestfield Cars is a new organisation. F

12 Chestfield Cars will go anywhere. T

13 A discount is available for bookings of eight or more. NG

MATCHING

Matching is a test of your skimming and scanning skills and it is important to develop these so that you are able to read quickly in order to find the information that you need.

IELTS Reading (GT)

How to approach the task

► Read through the list of statements (Questions 14–20) and highlight the key words that will help you find the correct review.

► Skim through each review and mark any possible areas that match statements 14–20.

► When you have skimmed through all the reviews, go back and decide which ones contain ideas that directly match the statements.

► If you have more than one possible answer, re-read the texts very carefully to see if you can decide which is correct and which expresses a different meaning. Although you may be able to match vocabulary items, the meaning could be quite different.

Questions 14–20

*Look at the reviews of running jackets **A–F** on the next page. Match the statements about the jackets (**14–20**) to the descriptions in the reviews.*

TEST TIP

There may be more than one answer for some questions of this type. If this is the case, the instructions will clearly explain this. Otherwise, you should only put one answer on your answer sheet.

14 This jacket will give you the greatest protection in bad weather. AC

15 This is the least expensive of the jackets. D

16 You can remove the hood of this jacket. C

17 The company that makes this jacket has come up with a new fabric. B

18 This jacket makes more noise when you run than any other jackets. A

19 You cannot buy this jacket at the moment. E

20 This is suitable as a fashion jacket too. F

 For further practice, do the Supplementary activity on page 114.

Follow-up

When you have finished this unit, you may move on to Reading Unit 2 *Skimming/scanning for specific information and detail.*

A Arlo Blockout £99.99

Features Double storm flap at front; adjustable velcro straps on sleeves; hood rolls away into collar.

Evaluation As the dropped tail, slightly heavier material and storm flaps show, this is not exclusively a running jacket. That doesn't mean you can't run in it. You can, although you feel and hear it a lot more than the others. The water-proofing is excellent, but it struggled to allow any air circulation on longer runs. But if you intend to do more than run in the jacket, this is the one for you.

B Fine World £84.99

Features Reflective piping on back of shoulders and logo on collar; detachable hood; two side pockets.

Evaluation Fine World set out with the intent of finding a fully waterproof, breathable material at an affordable price. It has largely achieved that with a coated nylon which is fairly light, reasonably quiet and certainly keeps out the water. Where it suffers is in its ability to keep you dry inside. The polyester lining was always soaking after every run, especially around the upper body.

C Fine Form £119.99

Features Concealed hood; front and back reflective trim; two side pockets.

Evaluation This is a classic, no-frills jacket specifically designed for the running market. It is heavier than some of the other models, but it's certainly the best one to be wearing in the midst of a storm. Due to the weight, you tend to generate more sweat when you're running, which it struggles to clear. It is expensive but well finished throughout. One minor irritant is the hood, which is bulky when rolled away in the collar and would be better detached.

D High Flyer £49.99

Features Reflective piping; half-body lining; two side pockets.

Evaluation If you want light and quiet, this is your jacket. The material must be one of the lightest around. It has a soft, cotton-like feel which cuts down on the usual noise of the jacket rubbing against itself. But while water initially beaded and fell off the jacket, in a heavy downpour it can become quite damp inside. However, it did dry out again particularly quickly. If you're worried about price, this is a good option.

E Run riot £79.99

Features Concealed hood; reflective piping; side pockets.

Evaluation Their new material, Vortex, is extremely light, fully waterproof and seems to breathe pretty well. Rather than just a warm-up jacket, this really is a model we felt you could train in. The all-round vents help the body breathe, and though the mesh lining was sometimes damp after a run, the outer material wasn't.

(NB The jacket is not available until next season.)

F Storm-trooper £119.99

Features Reflective trim on body and sleeves; elasticated Velcro cuffs; thick collar.

Evaluation Despite its appearance, Storm-trooper's weatherproof material has a soft feel. However, although the large back vents help air circulate, it doesn't keep you perfectly dry inside, and the fleecy collar doesn't help. Nevertheless, everyone who ran in the jacket liked it a lot. In fact, it looked almost too good to go out running in. The one curious thing is the colour. Despite the reflective elements, near-black is a strange choice for a winter jacket.

Reading

Section 2 of the General Training module also tests your ability to retrieve factual information and the task types that you may come across will be similar to those in Section 1.

1 What is the general theme of the texts in Section 2?

2 How many words will you have to read in Section 2?

MATCHING

One of the texts in Section 2 may be made up of smaller texts. Look at the advertisements on the next page. Skim through the information to get a general idea of the content.

3 What are the advertisements for?

4 How many residences are expensive?

When you skim through a text like this the first time, it is a good idea to make use of any graphics, keys and all headings/titles etc. to help you get an overview of the content.

IELTS Reading (GT)

Answer Questions 5–9 by writing the appropriate telephone numbers in boxes 5–9 on your answer sheet.

NB *You may use any number more than once.*

Which number would you ring if you are interested in

5 a double room and full board at a reasonable price?

6 long-term single accommodation with sports facilities?

7 inexpensive accommodation for yourself and your family?

8 low-budget, furnished accommodation for yourself and your partner?

9 a room close to the university with linen and laundry included?

 For further practice, do the Supplementary activity on page 114.

Student Accommodation Guide

Banbury House** Tel: 564839

Enjoy mixing with other students in luxury accommodation 30 minutes from the station and close to all main bus routes. Single and double rooms. Students provide own food but all cleaning services offered. Please bring your own linen.

Home from Home** Tel: 567233

Single or underline(double rooms) for students. Fully air-conditioned with all amenities. Only a few minutes on foot to the city centre and close to colleges. All services and meals included. The management do not provide room-mates for individuals seeking double occupancy.

full board

Three Seasons* Tel: 445987

We can provide all types of accommodation for all types of single student. Rooms are fully furnished with linen and have reasonable rates. Full board possible. 35–40 minutes from main universities and city. Please observe codes of conduct.

Downtown Digs* Tel: 882312

Do you worry that you'll not have enough money to see the term through? Don't waste it on expensive housing. This is a hostel for students run by students. No references and no rules. Shared bathroom, dormitory accommodation.

Must provide own linen. All cleaning operates on a rota system. Singles only.

Sturtin Hostel*** Tel: 876333

We offer scenic views and old-world charm. Located in pleasant rural surroundings. Relax after a long day by swimming in the pool or using the exercise gym. Separate study rooms available. No children. Bar & restaurant.

Star Lodgings* Tel: 322756

This is a hotel but it offers apartment style housing so that you can retain some independence. Single or double rooms available with separate bathroom. All unfurnished. Children welcome.

First stop* Tel: 223300

Ideal for new students, we provide double rooms. If you wish, we can offer assistance in finding a suitable person to share a room with. All washing and cleaning services offered at extra charge. Large canteen and three bathrooms on each floor. Sports centre next door.

Highdown House** Tel: 919102

Bed and breakfast hotel offers student accommodation for limited period only. Vacancies for on-the-spot reservations usually available. Own bathroom and laundry facilities but no cooking on premises. Sports room and small pool.

KEY   * cheap   ** reasonable   *** expensive

Take note!!

PARAGRAPH HEADINGS

Reading Section 2 may also test your global reading skills. Look at the IELTS activity below and the passage on the following page.

IELTS Reading

How to approach the task (class activity)

► Skim through the passage once to get a general idea of what it is about.
► Read it a second time and underline any key words or ideas in Paragraph A.
► Discuss why *x* is the correct heading for this paragraph and all the others are wrong.
► Go on to Paragraph B. Discuss the key ideas and then select the best heading for this paragraph.
► Do the rest of the exercise on your own.

*The Reading Passage on the following page has six paragraphs **A–F**.*

*Choose the most suitable heading for each paragraph from the list of headings below. Write the appropriate letters (**i–x**) in boxes 10–14 on your answer sheet.*

NB   There are more headings than paragraphs so you will not use all of them. You may use any heading more than once.

TEST TIP
Although there may be a number of ideas together in a paragraph, the task is to select the heading that covers the main topic/theme.

List of Headings

i	Unexpected growth
ii	How it all started
iii	When to pick the right course
iv	Making demands
v	The participants
vi	First attempts
vii	Factors influencing school leavers
viii	Focus on equality
ix	Higher education needs
x	A hard choice

Example	*Answer*
Paragraph A	x

10 Paragraph B   ii   **13** Paragraph E   ×

11 Paragraph C   √   **14** Paragraph F   viii

12 Paragraph D   i

Visit to Student Fair is Vital Homework

A The number and variety of courses on offer these days makes it difficult to pick the right one. But thousands of Europeans who flock to Brussels Exhibition Centre will be shown how to simplify the difficult job of choosing the right course of study for the career they wish to pursue.

B Ten years ago a handful of Belgian teenagers, baffled by the array and number of university courses on offer, put their heads together to try to hack their way through the academic undergrowth. They knew that choosing the wrong subject or failing to make the grade would make finding a job all the more difficult. They decided something had to be done to help students approach the task of choosing a course in an effective way. They came up with the idea of a Student Fair.

C It was decided that this would take the form of a small forum for everyone in Belgium involved in higher education from both the French and Dutch-speaking parts of the country. It would provide the opportunity for representatives of educational institutions to give information on the courses they have on offer and allow school-leavers time to discuss these with them.

D But what the youngsters did not know was that they were tapping a source of anxiety among students right across Europe. The fair became an annual event. It expanded to include higher education bodies from the whole continent, becoming known as the European Student Fair.

E 'Each year ten million students are faced with the same dilemma,' said exhibition organiser Valerie de Norre. 'The bewildering variety of options, the evolution of the employment market, the economic downturn, changes in working methods and personal interests all play an important role in the decision-making process. We hope the fair can help people make the correct decision for themselves.'

F This year the theme of the fair is 'the right to education for all' and to mark this there is a special exhibition area for bodies that promote equal opportunities in education. Also, the Master of Business Administration course continues to attract an enormous amount of interest across Europe and, in response to demand, fair organisers are once again holding an MBA day.

Follow-up

For further practice in this task, go to Reading Unit 4 *Improving global reading skills*.

PART 3

In order to prepare for General Training Reading Section 3, you should cover Reading Units 1, 5, 6 and 7.

The Writing Module

GENERAL WRITING STRATEGIES

As a student at college or university, you will have to produce a lot of written material. Some of this may be in the form of short essays or reports. Other pieces of writing will be longer and will require considerable planning and attention to detail. It will therefore be important for you to be able to express yourself clearly, write in a variety of styles and organise your ideas carefully. You will also need to be fairly accurate in your writing, so that your message is not obscured by a lot of grammatical errors.

IELTS WRITING (ACADEMIC)

IELTS tests your ability to produce two quite different pieces of writing in a fairly short period of time. The test is divided into two parts and you are allowed one hour to complete both parts.

Writing Task 1

In the first part, you are given a task based on some graphic or pictorial information. You are expected to write a descriptive report of at least 150 words on the information provided.

Writing Task 2

The second task is more demanding. You are expected to produce a written argument on a given topic and to organise your answer clearly, giving some examples to support your points. You will have to write at least 250 words and, as Task 2 is longer than Task 1, you are advised to spend approximately 40 minutes on this task and 20 minutes on the first task.

IELTS WRITING (GENERAL TRAINING)

If you are planning to take the GT module, the Writing test is different. You are allowed one hour to complete two tasks, of 150 and 250 words, as in the Academic module. However, Task 1 is always a letter, while Task 2 is an essay based on a given topic.

If you are studying for the General Training module, you should begin with Writing Units 5 and 6.

Writing

UNIT 1 Describing facts and figures

Being able to understand and describe graphic information or data is an important academic skill. IELTS Academic Writing Task 1 tests your ability to describe factual information, presented in graphic and diagrammatic form, clearly and accurately.

BAR CHARTS

A fact is different from an opinion because it is objective and often involves measurement. For example, the graph on the right shows what a group of students think about a film they have just seen.

Having looked at this graph, you could say that *half the students did not like the film*. Or you could say that *50 per cent of the students did not like the film. You could be even more specific and state that 15 out of 30 students did not like the film*. These are all facts.

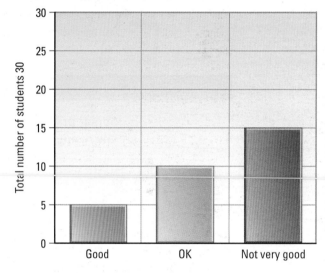

- Find out some factual information about your class members or your friends and family. How many of them enjoy taking part in the following activities? Put a tick against each activity the people like doing and then write the total in the *Total* column. Then turn the table into a bar chart.
- Make some factual statements about the data. Try to use all the following structures:
  number (e.g. five out of ten) students enjoy ...
  percentage (e.g. 50 per cent of) students enjoy ...
  general (e.g. the majority of / a large number of / most / very few / hardly any) students enjoy ...

Activity	Total
Martial arts	
Singing	
Computer games	
Running	
Cooking	
Climbing	

 For more practice in describing graphs, do Exercise A in the Supplementary activities on page 115.

PIE CHARTS

- Look at this pie chart, which shows how a young woman called Tomoko spends her money.
- Look at the sentences below that have been written about the pie chart. See if you can correct them.

1 Tomoko spends an equal amount of money on rent, food, study materials and entertainment.

2 Tomoko spends 45 per cent of her money on rent and food, but she only spends 15 per cent of her money on study materials.

3 Tomoko spends more on clothes than she spends on study materials.

4 Tomoko spends as much money on rent and food as she does on everything else put together.

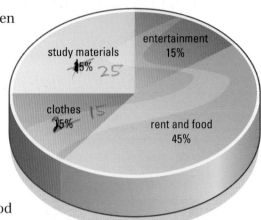

study materials
15% *25*

entertainment
15%

clothes
15% *15*

rent and food
45%

 For further practice, do Exercise B in the Supplementary activities on page 115.

TABLES

- A popular magazine conducted a survey about their readers' smoking habits. Here are the results:

Cigarette smoking habits *by gender %*			
	all	*men*	*women*
20 + a day	11	13	9
10–19 a day	11	11	10
less than 10 a day	8	7	10
given up	27	30	24
never smoked	43	39	47

Complete the following sentences which describe some of the facts in the table.

5 ....*43 per cent of*...... the readers have never smoked.

6 Almost a third of the readers ......*used to smoke*............ but have now given up.

7 A ....*relatively small quantage*..........*8 per cent*............. of readers smoke less than ten cigarettes a day.

8 Generally speaking, men are ......*heavier smokers*....... than women.

9 ......*The percentage*.............. of readers who smoke more than twenty a day is quite small, at 11 per cent overall.

10 The figures for the 20-plus group and the 10–19 group ......*are similar*............ .

Writing

UNIT 2 Describing trends

Line graphs are used to show a trend or pattern which usually takes place over a period of time. It is important to look at the overall pattern on a line graph as well as the significant features within it.

LINE GRAPHS

1 What information is being shown in the graph below?

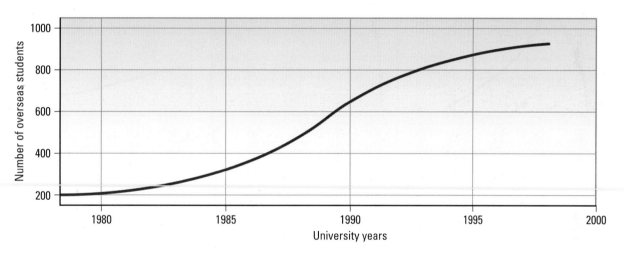

2 Here are two simple descriptions of the graph:

The number of overseas students studying at the university has risen. **Or**
The graph shows an increase in the number of overseas students at the university.

Add 'considerably' to the first sentence and 'considerable' to the second sentence. What effect does this word have?

3 Here are some words and phrases to help you describe trends:

nouns	adjectives and adverbs	phrase
a rise	sharp(ly) / dramatic(ally)	remain the same
an increase	considerable(ly)	reach a plateau
a fall	steady(ily)	remain stable
a drop	slight(ly) / gentle(ly)	remain/stay constant
a decline	gradual(ly)	reach a peak
a peak/dip	relative(ly)	hit/fall to the lowest point

Using some of the words and phrases on the previous page, describe the pattern in each graph below.

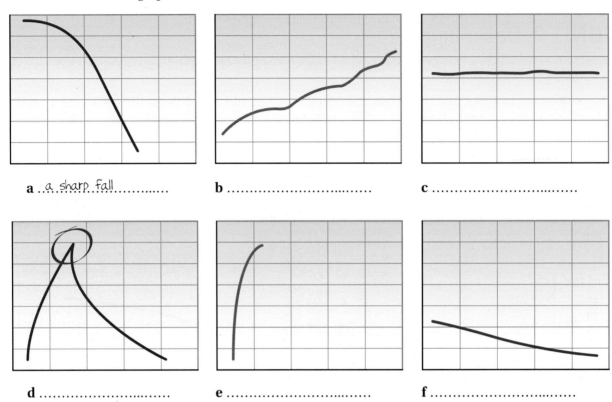

a ..a sharp fall...........

b ....

c ....

d ....

e ....

f ....

4 Describe each pattern using a verb, e.g. **a** *It falls sharply.*

EXAMINING THE AXES

This trend looks very simple but **think about** it before you describe it.

5 Is the graph about **people** or **vehicles**?

6 What do the numbers along the horizontal axis represent?

7 What do the numbers on the vertical axis represent?

8 Write a **short**, **general** statement about car ownership in Britain.

9 Now include the time period. Use:

   a *since 1960* **b** *(over a 40-year period) between 1960 and 2000*

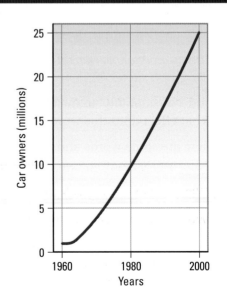

10 Now include the number of car owners in both sentences. (This may mean that you have to re-organise your sentence.)

11 Write a fuller description of the graph at the beginning of this unit.

 For further practice, do Exercise A in the Supplementary activities on page 115.

12 Write one sentence that describes what each of the graphs below is about. Then describe the trends that you can see in each graph.

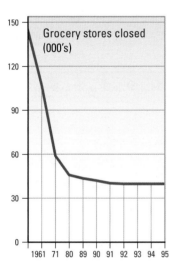

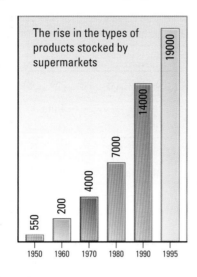

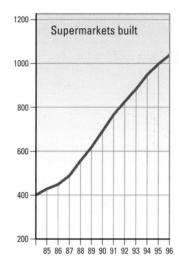

13 What does the graph below show?

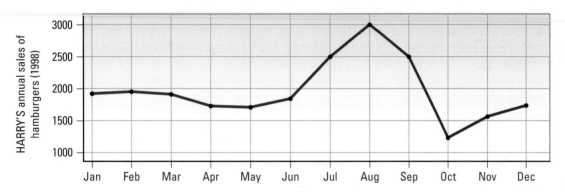

14 How is this graph different from the ones you have looked at so far?

15 Why do you think this information was presented on a line graph?

16 What tense will you use to describe it?

17 Write four sentences about the trends you can see in the above graph. See how many different types of structures your class can produce and write them all down. Practise using the words *stable, fewer, rise, sales, peak, drop, popular.*

TEST TIP

You could write twelve sentences about this graph — one for each month. But if you do that you will not be describing the 'trends' and your answer will be very repetitive. Your examiner will be checking to see whether you can describe the important features of the graph.

Follow-up

- What is being shown in the graph below?

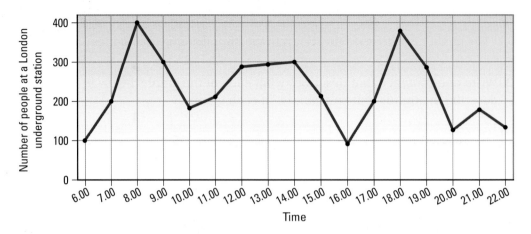

- Read the following description of the graph above.

At 6 a.m. the station had 100 people. At 8 a.m. it had a big increase to 400 people. Not many people were there at 10 a.m. The same thing happened after 8 p.m. It declined a lot to 120 and 180 people at 9 p.m. and 10 p.m. respectively. Between 12 noon and 2 p.m. the number of people was stabilised at 300.

- Discuss what is wrong with the above paragraph, then write your own paragraph, making improvements. A model answer, one of many possible versions, is given on page 182.

 For further practice, do the IELTS task, Exercise B of the Supplementary activities on page 116.

Writing

UNIT 3 Summarising data

In the IELTS test there may be a lot of information to describe, in a limited number of words. It is essential that you select the appropriate details and organise the material in a relevant way in order to fulfil the task requirements satisfactorily.

SELECTING IMPORTANT INFORMATION

- Examine the graph below carefully.

Mobile phone owner growth

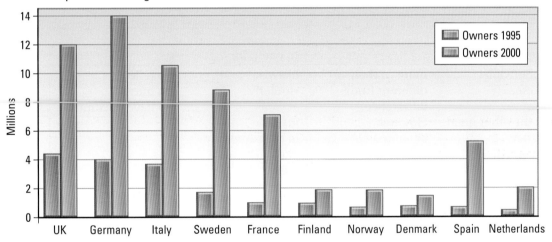

1 Write one sentence which says what the graph shows.

2 Write two sentences which give *overall* information about the graph.

3 Write a fourth sentence about France.

4 Write a fifth sentence about the UK.

5 Write a final sentence about Germany.

- Exchange your answers with a partner and discuss the features you chose to describe. Then look at the sample answer in the Key on page 182.

TEST TIP

This graph does not provide information about population size. If you choose to include information in your answer that is not given in the task, you will not get extra marks. In fact, it may be considered irrelevant (and penalised) if you make detailed comments about information that is not provided in the diagram.

Follow-up

- Discuss the important features of the following graph.

Average book prices, in pounds sterling – statistics published by the Policy Studies Institute

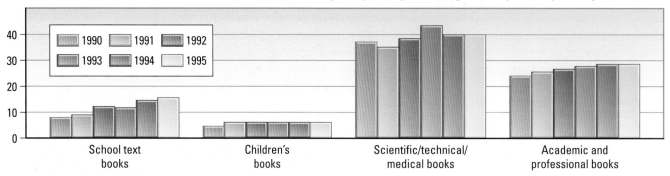

COMPARING DATA

When you interpret graphs, tables and charts, you will find that you have to *compare* and *contrast* some of the details. Your examiner will be checking that you can *structure* your answer well and *connect* your ideas appropriately. The following table may help you do this.

to contrast		to compare	
while/whilst	more ... than	likewise	to reflect
whereas	different from	similarly	to mirror
however	differ(ence)	as ... as	to have in common
on the other hand	although	just as	
even so	in contrast to	in the same way	
nevertheless	conversely	like	
less ... than	unlike	alike	

- Look at the following diagram.

Running events

sprints

100m
10.49sec

1500m
3min
50.45sec

9.95 sec

+6.1%

Marathon
2hr 21min
6sec

2min
27.37
sec

+10%

24hr
154 miles

2hrs
6min
50sec

+10%

6 days
548 miles

178
miles

+15.6%

640
miles

+16.8%

- Complete the gaps in the following paragraph that describes the diagram on the previous page.

  Generally speaking men are (**6**) .... women in running events. The gap is greatest in the long-distance events and (**7**) .... in the sprints. In the six-day running event, the best male runners can cover 640 miles, (**8**) .... the fastest women cover only 548 miles. This represents a difference of 16.8 per cent. This difference becomes (**9**) .... significant in the shorter events. In the 100m, for example, there is only a 6.1 per cent (**10**) .... in performance between men and women.

- Compare some of the other details on this diagram.

GROUPING INFORMATION

When organising your answer it may also help to 'group' some of the information. This is particularly the case when there is a lot of data, as in the graph on the right.

Here there are too many age groups for each to be described independently, so it helps to group some of them.

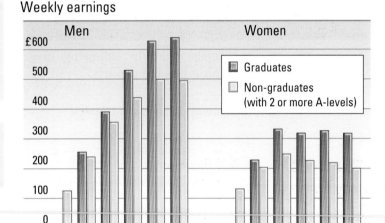

Weekly earnings

- **How to approach the task**
  - ► Consider what the graph shows and think about the vocabulary and tenses you will use in describing it.
  - ► Select two significant features of the graph (overall) to write about.
  - ► Note some points about the earning power of female graduates by grouping the ages 25–59.
  - ► Note some points about the male graduates by grouping the ages as you feel is appropriate.
  - ► Consider the comparisons you will make.
  - ► Think about a final point.

TEST TIP

You will lose marks in IELTS if you interpret the important information inaccurately, however correct your answer may be grammatically.

- Now write a paragraph describing the information shown in the graph.

 For further practice, do the IELTS Supplementary activity on page 117.

Writing

UNIT 4 Describing a process

TEST TIP

It is important to avoid copying the task as examiners will simply ignore any material copied from the test paper and you will get no credit for this.

In Writing Task 1 you may occasionally be asked to describe a process or other pictorial information such as a cycle or map. In order to produce a report describing a process you should take a similar approach to the one you used in describing data. You should examine the information carefully – which will be in pictorial form – and make sure you understand it. Look specifically at the beginning and the end of the process. Then, following the same principles as outlined in previous units, you should provide an opening sentence that summarises the *overall* function of the process.

 1 Discuss what the following diagram is about. Then write a sentence which summarises the process.

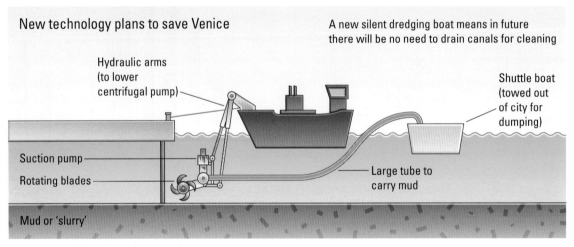

New technology plans to save Venice

A new silent dredging boat means in future there will be no need to drain canals for cleaning

Hydraulic arms (to lower centrifugal pump)

Shuttle boat (towed out of city for dumping)

Suction pump

Rotating blades

Large tube to carry mud

Mud or 'slurry'

- Describe the process verbally to each other. See if you agree on the facts. Then write your description of the process in 20 minutes.

How to approach the task

TEST TIP

If necessary, you can jot down a few notes on the answer sheet. These can be crossed out when you have finished and will not be marked.

- ► List some of the verbs that you will use in your answer.
- ► Suggest some suitable connectives. What should you avoid doing when you link the stages in the process?
- ► Decide what tenses you will use. What does this depend on?

- Compare your description with your partner's. Look particularly at the verbs and connectors that he/she has used.

There are various ways that you can respond to this task and the sample answer in the Answer Key is one example.

IELTS Writing (Academic)   **Task 1**

You should spend about 20 minutes on this task.

> ***The diagram below shows how the water cycle works.***
>
> ***Write a report for a university lecturer describing the information shown.***

You should write at least 150 words.

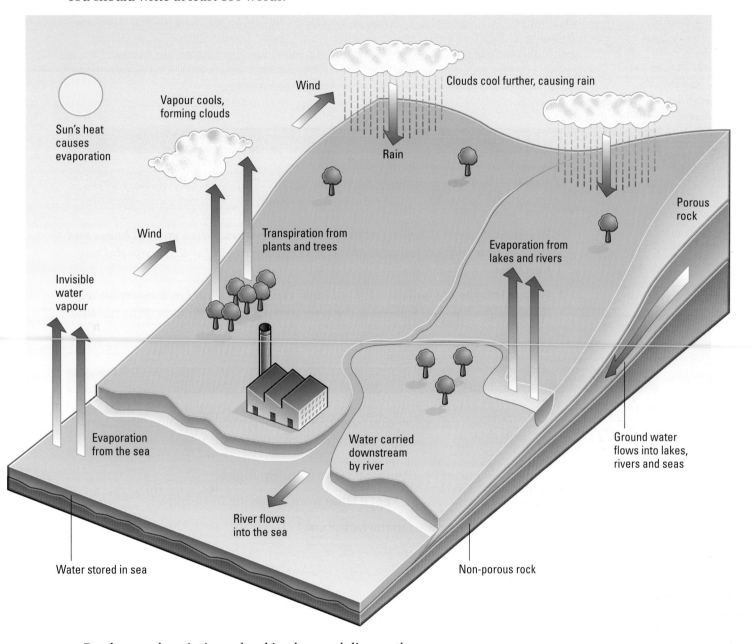

- Read some descriptions aloud in class and discuss them.

 For further practice, do the Supplementary activity on page 117.

Writing

Letters are an important form of communication. In the General Training Writing Task 1 you are given a situation and tested on your ability to write a letter in an appropriate style in order to achieve a certain outcome. You need to include all the necessary details so that the purpose of your letter is clear and the reader can easily understand your message.

THE TASK

The task will present a situation to you on the question paper. You have to write in the first person and imagine yourself in the situation given. Here is an example:

You recently went shopping at the local supermarket. When you got home and studied your bill you found that you had been charged for items you did not purchase.

Write a letter to the supermarket manager explaining what has happened. Tell the manager how you feel about the error and ask him to do something about it.

1 Underline the verbs in this task which express what you have to do.

THE PURPOSE

It is important to remember that a letter is a form of communication. Formal or semi-formal letters are always written with a particular purpose in mind.

2 What is really meant by a 'purpose'? Give some examples.

3 What sort of things may prevent a letter from achieving its purpose?

4 What purpose is intended in the task above?

Starting out

The purpose is sometimes stressed at the beginning of a letter. (It depends on the type of letter you are writing as to how much you emphasise your purpose at the start or whether you decide to leave it to the end of the letter.) However, you do need to open your letter with something that will be appropriate for the reader and will capture the reader's attention and there are structures to help you do this. Read the following examples:

I am writing with regard/reference to/in connection with ...
I am writing to express my concern/dissatisfaction about ...
I would like to draw your attention to ...

5 What sort of tone do these structures have?

6 How might you begin a letter of apology to a friend?

• Discuss the purpose of each of the following letters.

> **7** A letter to the gas company about a second bill (or reminder) you received when you had already paid the first.

> **8** A letter to a close relative with an invitation to a surprise party.

> **9** A letter to an old teacher asking for a reference for a job.

> **10** A letter to a garage about some poor mechanical work they did on your car.

• Write an opening sentence or sentences for the above letters, then discuss these with your teacher.

EXPLAINING THE SITUATION

It is important that any background you provide on the situation is clear and includes all the information the reader needs.

• Re-read the first paragraph of the task on page 78 and look at the ideas in the bubble diagram below.

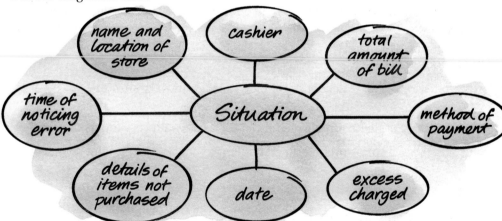

TEST TIP

It is worth reading the question several times to make sure you understand it fully, as you will lose marks in IELTS if you ~~misinterpret the~~ situation.

• Write the first part of your letter giving an explanation of what happened at the supermarket. (You will write the second half of the letter in Writing Unit 6.)

How to approach the task

► You will need to invent some information for this task. You must use your imagination but make sure your ideas are realistic and fit the situation.

► Copy this diagram and replace the ideas in the bubbles with realistic information.

► Consider the order in which you would want to present the information in a letter.

► Consider the tenses you will use.

Writing

Once you have your purpose clearly in mind and have given the reader some background information, you should continue with your message. The tone and level of formality that you use in your letter will affect how successful you are at communicating your message.

THE MESSAGE

Expressing feelings

There are many feelings that you may wish to convey in a letter. Here are some of the vocabulary and structures associated with them.

Dissatisfaction/dislike	Regret/apology	Needs/wants/desires
I am unhappy about/do not like …	I'm sorry that I …	What I am looking for is …
I am not comfortable about/with …	I regret that I …	What would suit me best is …
… is not what I expected/was expecting.	Please accept my apologies for …ing	I am very keen to …
… does not suit me/my needs.	Please forgive me for …	I would very much like to …
… is too + adjective	Unfortunately/Regrettably I …	I would be grateful if you could …
Gratitude	**Annoyance**	**Pleasure/satisfaction**
Thank you very much for …	Although I stated that …	I was delighted about/by …
I very much appreciated …	Despite my request for …	I thoroughly enjoyed …
I'm grateful to you for …	Even though I telephoned you about …	… was very impressive/enjoyable.

1 What other feelings might you want to express in a letter?

Making requests, suggestions, etc.

You may also have to request or suggest something in your letter.

2 Look at the list of sentences and expressions below. What do you notice about those in the left-hand column?

3 Discuss with your teacher how a reader would react to some of the statements in the left-hand column.

- Rewrite some of the messages in the left-hand column using a structure from the right-hand column.

Send me a brochure.	I would like to ...
I want a ticket for tonight's show.	I am very interested in ...ing
I think you should employ more staff.	Could I suggest that ...
You should give up smoking.	Please avoid ...ing
In my opinion you should improve your service.	Wouldn't it be better if you ...
I want to get a place at your school.	I would be grateful if you/I could ...
I can't stand your car alarm.	Please would you ... /Could you please ...
You park your car too close to mine.	I would recommend that you ...
Why is your information always out-of-date?	I would appreciate it if ...

- Write the second part of your letter in which you state how you feel about the supermarket error and ask the manager to do something about it. (See pages 78–79.)

IELTS Writing (GT)   Task 1

You should spend about 20 minutes on this task.

You have a friend who lives in a city abroad. You have decided that you would like to apply to do a course at one of the colleges in this city.

Write to your friend explaining what you would like to do. Tell him/her what type of work or studies you have been doing for the past few years and ask for assistance in contacting an appropriate institution.

You should write at least 150 words.
You do NOT need to write your own address.

Begin your letter as follows:

Dear ......,

- A model answer, one of many possible approaches, is given on page 186.

 For more letter-writing practice, do the Supplementary activity on page 118.

TEST TIP
You must respond to each point mentioned in the task. If you leave something out, you will lose marks.

TASK 2

To prepare for General Training Task 2, you should study Writing Units 7–11.

Writing

See what you can remember about Writing Task 2 from your reading of the introduction to the Writing module on page 66.

1 How many words are you expected to write?

2 How long should you spend on the task?

3 What sort of writing are you expected to produce?

4 What must you include in your answer?

5 What sort of things do you think the examiners will be checking for?

UNDERSTANDING THE INSTRUCTIONS

There are no 'right' or 'wrong' answers to this task, but you must read the question carefully and make sure you understand exactly what you have to write about.

The introduction to Writing Task 2 is as follows:

TEST TIP

You will lose marks if you misunderstand the question, write about something not required in the question, or address only half or less of the topic. For this reason it is worth spending a little time analysing the question.

Academic
Present a written argument or case to an educated reader with no specialist knowledge of the following topic:

OR *General Training*
As part of a class assignment you have to write about the following topic:

• What sort of answer do you think you should write?

After the task, the instructions state:

Academic
You should use your own ideas, knowledge and experience and support your arguments with examples and relevant evidence.

OR *General Training*
Give reasons for your answer.

• How should you approach the task?

APPROACHING THE TASK

- Read the following task.

    Enormous effort is put into researching and marketing 'the perfect potato crisp' while research into stress at work, for example, is ignored.

    How important are staff working conditions? Should employers research and improve the working conditions of their staff or should they concentrate more on their product?

6 Which of the following areas would it be appropriate to include in your answer?

   a a comparison of different types of product
   b a discussion of the difficulties of food industries
   c an analysis of the effects of bad working environments
   d an explanation of how to make potato crisps
   e an analysis of how to be successful in business
   f a description of a business you know well
   g an analysis of the importance of a company's product
   h a discussion of how products are manufactured
   i a discussion of the value of company staff

 - Read the task below and discuss with your partner what it means and what it is asking you to write about.

    The age of Information Technology has taken a lot of people by surprise. While it has become a way of life for some, others know very little about it and may be unlikely to learn. Eventually we will have a polarised society and this will lead to serious social problems.

    To what extent do you agree with this statement?

- Write some examples (as in **a–i** above) of the areas you might cover in an answer. Do not feel that you must agree with the argument put forward in the question.
- Try to re-write the task in your own words.

- On your own, write your answer simply and clearly in about 250 words.

FORMING IDEAS

Your examiner will expect you to present *clearly* a number of *relevant* ideas in your answer.

You can develop ideas on a topic that has a central theme by *brainstorming*. Before you turn over, take a look again at the bubble diagram on page 79.

- Get into groups of two to four students and discuss this statement:

   Children over 15 should be allowed to make decisions about their lives without the interference of their parents or teachers. Society should accept that children mature at a younger age these days and should adjust the law accordingly.

   Discuss this statement in relation to your own society or a society that you know well.

- As you develop ideas, get one member of your group to complete a bubble diagram on an OHP transparency.
- When you have finished, look at the diagrams that your class has produced. Discuss some of them and see whether your classmates have come up with any different ideas.

   Another way of developing your ideas on a topic that has two sides is to make a list of 'pros' and 'cons' or points 'for' and 'against'.

- Read the following question.

   Have newspapers become a medium of the past or do they still play an important role in people's lives?

- This time work on your own. Get a new sheet of paper and draw a line down the middle of it like this:

For	Against
cheap to buy	time-consuming to read
detailed information	waste of paper

TEST TIP
If you focus on a very limited aspect of the topic, you will lose marks because you have not analysed the topic sufficiently. You will also lose marks if you do not write the required number of words.

- See what ideas you can come up with.
- Compare your ideas with those of others in your class.
- Produce a complete class list for each side of the argument.
- Write up your answer in 250 words.

 For more practice on developing ideas, do the Supplementary activity on page 118.

Writing

In the examination you will have very little time to plan your answer, but your examiner will be looking for a clear underlying structure in your response.

1 What do you think is meant by a 'clear underlying structure'?

ORGANISING IDEAS

> The key to good, clear writing is simplicity. Do not start the introduction until you know what you are going to say in your answer. Once you have thought of some relevant ideas, you need to *organise* them. If you produce an answer that presents a list of ideas without development, you will lose marks.

2 What do you think is involved in organising your ideas?

3 What will happen to some of your ideas?

- Spend ten minutes doing a 'for/against' activity (see page 84) on the following topic.

  > ***Should parents be obliged to immunise their children against common childhood diseases? Or do individuals have the right to choose not to immunise their children?***

- Now organise your ideas in preparation for writing the answer (which you will be asked to do at the end of this Unit).

How to approach the task

- ► Decide which of the ideas in your lists are 'key' ideas. (You may not agree on this, so try to argue your case.)
- ► Discuss how many of the key ideas you think you could cover in 250 words.
- ► Take a new sheet of paper and divide it into columns so that you have one column for each key idea. Discuss what order you think the ideas should go in. Write the key ideas at the top of each column in the order you have decided.
- ► Select some supporting points for each key idea from your lists. Write these beneath the relevant key idea.
- ► Think about your own experience and consider if you have any further supporting points to add.

- On your own, get a new sheet of paper and write down all your ideas on the following topic. Then plan your key ideas and supporting points. Do this in ten minutes.

  As children do we have a natural ability and motivation to take up new interests (such as languages, sports and musical instruments) which as adults we seem to lose? Are there too many social pressures on adults or are there other reasons for the apparent decline in a human being's capacity to learn?

THE INTRODUCTION

Your introduction is very important because it gives your reader their first impression of your writing ability. However, you shouldn't begin your introduction immediately.

4 What must you decide before you write the introduction?

5 Roughly how long should the introduction to an IELTS answer be?

6 Roughly how long should you spend writing the introduction?

7 How should you indicate the end of the introduction to your reader?

TEST TIP

If you copy the task word for word, you will be wasting time as the examiner will just ignore this part of your answer.

Your approach to writing an introduction will depend to a certain extent on the task. IELTS tasks present a discussion topic that is fairly broad and can be approached by candidates from different backgrounds. So one of the things you need to do in the introduction is to define what you understand by the task and state how you intend to approach it.

- Read the following task and discuss what areas you could cover in your answer and how you might introduce the topic.

  A company in which every employee is made to feel important will run more smoothly and experience greater success than a company that values some employees above others. Discuss.

8 Underline words or ideas that you feel are open to different interpretations. One approach you can take in an introduction is to pose questions that you then explore in the main body of your answer. What kind of questions could you pose in this introduction?

9 Consider your opinion about the statement presented in the task. An introduction can include a sentence stating the writer's position on the topic (but this is not essential). How could you state your position on this topic?

10 Write an introduction to the topic.

There is a model paragraph in the Answer Key. Remember that this model answer is just *one* example of how you could introduce this topic.

 The Supplementary activity on page 119 presents two more examples of opening paragraphs to this topic which you may discuss.

THE CONCLUSION

Like the introduction, an answer that does not include a conclusion is also incomplete. Your conclusion is important because it summarises your views for the reader.

11 Roughly how long should the conclusion to an IELTS answer be?

12 How should you indicate the start of the conclusion to your reader?

Your conclusion should summarise the key ideas that you wrote about and your views on these, resulting in a final verdict/decision/statement, if appropriate. You can also be impartial (i.e. take no side) or state that you have no conclusion to draw.

Structures like these can be useful in a conclusion:

To sum up   *In conclusion*
Overall   *To conclude*
In the final analysis *Ultimately*

- Look at the following model answer to the task at the top of page 86. Highlight the key ideas in it and then write an appropriate conclusion in approximately 40 words.

It is undoubtedly true that children are often well motivated to learn. However, does this motivation fade naturally as they develop or does society put pressures on the individual that interfere with successful learning?

It can generally be observed that children are better at learning than adults. They will more readily take up a musical instrument, for example, than a parent and are more likely to persist in mastering it.

Why is this so? It seems that while children have the determination to practise, adults are less patient. This suggests that we expect to pick things up far more quickly than is realistic. In addition, adults have more commitments than the young and so perhaps they lack the time to persist with their studies.

However, if it were true that it is only the pace of life that inhibits our learning capacity, this would imply that the busier we are, the less likely we would be to take up new interests. In my experience, this is not generally the case.

To sum up, enthusiasm for learning new things seems to be dependent on the individual concerned, rather than on their lifestyle. In fact it is common to find people who lead active lives or have demanding jobs taking up hobbies and other activities as well.

- Write up your answer to the first topic in this unit on immunisation. Compare your answer with the models on page 185 in the Answer Key.

Writing

In Writing Task 2, you are being tested on your ability to produce a clear, logical argument. The General Training task may require more description than argument, but this should still be clearly presented.

EXPRESSING VIEWS

Your key ideas will form the basis of your argument. Often they can simply be stated as facts, but if you want to personalise your argument, the following structures can help you reinforce what is *your* opinion or show that you are giving a *general* opinion.

I would argue that	*People argue that*
I (firmly) believe that	*Some people think/say that*
It seems to me that	*It is understood that*
I tend to think that	*It is generally accepted that*

- Write a sentence expressing one of your main ideas/opinions on the following:

  a teenage drivers are unsafe   **c** school uniforms should be compulsory

  b air travel should cost less   **d** books will soon be old-fashioned

- Read some sentences aloud in class. Did the writer use an appropriate structure? If not, why not?

MAKING CONCESSIONS

Another way of putting forward an argument without being too dogmatic, is to admit that there are arguments that differ from your own. Linking words and expressions such as *while, although, despite the fact that* are useful in doing this. Also adverbs such as *admittedly, certainly,* etc. can be used. Look at the following arguments for and against some well-known topics:

Topic	For	Against
A TV and children	Educational programmes – safe 'baby-sitting'	Adverts targeted at children – too much violence
B Women working *versus* staying at home	Children benefit from nurseries and day-care	Young children need to be with their mothers
C Too many cars in cities	Build more roads	More car users

- In each case, imagine that your opinion is the 'against' argument. Write a short paragraph on each topic. Begin with a sentence containing the main argument and then clarify your view by making a concession. Here is an example:

> As far as I can tell, television has few benefits for children. While I agree that there are some good educational programmes these days, far too much advertising is targeted at children and this makes television viewing very undesirable.

Concessional structures are also useful for conclusions and summing up ideas.

REFUTING AN ARGUMENT

This is a forceful way of expressing an argument and is done by rejecting an argument that you do not agree with. The following are examples of structures that can be used to reject an argument:

I am unconvinced that   *It is hard to accept that*   *It is unjustifiable to*
I don't believe that   *There is little evidence*   *say that*
                        to support the … that

- See if you can express a view on the following topics, by rejecting the first argument (**a**) and then asserting the second argument (**b**), e.g.

I don't believe that politicians should be paid high salaries. They are simply employed to do a job like anybody else.

a politicians should be paid high salaries	**b** a job like anybody else
a internet a useful resource for children	**b** too much uncensored material
a running is good for you	**b** many physical injuries
a gambling should be banned	**b** useful revenue in tax

DEFINING/EXPLAINING

Sometimes it is necessary to explain what we mean more clearly. Look at the following:

> I would argue that many people today spend too much money on leisure. By this I mean that they seem unable to enjoy themselves without having to pay for their entertainment by, for example, hiring videos or going to the cinema.

Defining is particularly useful when you want to make your argument clearer or when you are using terms that may have many possible interpretations. The structures below can be helpful in doing this:

By ... I mean	*In other words*	*To be more precise*
By this I mean	*That is to say*	*Here I'm (not) referring to*

- Add another sentence to the following arguments using an expression from above:
  a In my opinion, extended families are more successful than nuclear families.
  b It is often said that young people are more tolerant than old people.
  c I am convinced that an element of choice is important in the school curriculum.
  d Job commitment is not always the key to success.

- Read some of your sentences aloud and discuss their structure and content.
- Read the following introduction to an IELTS question on the topic ***Examinations serve no useful purpose*** and identify the writer's techniques in explaining his/her argument:

> I am convinced that examinations have a positive influence on learning and by that I mean that they lead to a better grasp of the subject, which is essential in areas such as medicine. While I admit that they can create undue pressure on students and can cause stress-related conditions, I would argue that these problems can be largely avoided if the approach to examinations is handled effectively by those concerned. Overall, students are motivated by examinations and this motivation can only benefit them.

1 How strong are the writer's views?

2 How would you develop this argument?

For further practice, do the Supplementary activity on page 119.

Writing

UNIT 10 Developing an argument

In Writing Task 2, your examiner will be looking for main arguments that are clearly well supported. You are even reminded of this in the instructions to the task.

MAKING THE MAIN ARGUMENT CLEAR

- Read the following paragraph from a student essay on *Why people commit crimes*.

> I don't really agree that we should try to understand why someone has committed a crime. I think criminals should be punished and that's it. It isn't fair on the victim. In addition I would like to comment that most criminals know what they are doing when they commit a crime. There are too many crimes these days. I don't think there were so many in the past.

1 Can you identify the main and supporting argument(s)?

2 What is the problem with this paragraph?

- Now read a paragraph from a different essay:

> I would always support any attempt to foster greater community spirit amongst neighbours. Clearly they can be very supportive towards one another in very practical ways: younger neighbours can assist those who are more elderly, or people can do things for each other when they go on holiday, like checking the mail. Regrettably though, many of us nowadays are simply too busy to make the effort and it's not unknown for people to go for months without ever speaking to a neighbour. I live in a block of flats myself and of the four households on my floor, I have only met one other occupant.

3 What do you think the question is?

4 Can you identify the main and supporting arguments?

5 What type of support is provided?

PROVIDING SUPPORT

There are many ways in which you can link your main and supporting arguments and your choice will depend upon:

○ the type of support – is it an example, a further argument, an anecdote, etc?

○ the style of writing – are you predicting something, making a comparison, etc?

○ the nature of the argument – is it a very personal argument or a general one?

The following structures are closely connected with giving support but many of the other structures covered in this section can also be used.

For example	*Indeed*	*If this is/were the case*	*In my experience*
For instance	*In fact*	*Firstly*	*Let me illustrate*
A good example of this is	*Of course*	*Naturally*	

Remember it is important to try and vary the words and structures you use.

- Link the following arguments using an appropriate expression from the list above. Use something different in each gap.

6 It is impossible to predict what type of holidays people will be taking in 100 years' time. We don't know, ... , whether space travel will be a realistic option in the future. .... , it is likely to completely transform our traditional view of a holiday.

7 I would contend that supermarkets are here to stay. .... in some countries they can offer so many products that it's hardly necessary to shop anywhere else. .... there are sometimes instances of local opposition, but this is usually overcome.

8 Statistics show that the worst drivers in the world are young men. .... as a driver, if you look closely at any car that is going too fast, overtaking at the wrong place or driving too close to the car in front, it will invariably have a teenager or young man in the driver's seat.

9 I strongly approve of the preservation of historical buildings. Too many have already been destroyed; .... in my home town, whole streets of beautiful regency houses were knocked down in order to build high-rise flats.

- Look at the notes below which a student has written in order to prepare a response to the topic: ***In the interests of public safety, dangerous sports should be banned.***

Topic	Main ideas	Support
not sure - think I agree presume sports such as mountaineering/rock climbing/caving	people get lost or trapped - rescue teams involved OK if rules etc. are obeyed but some people irresponsible	rescue teams risk lives/have families ref. news last week, rescuer died

- Write the introduction and first paragraph of the answer.
- Plan a second paragraph that argues against the topic.
- Write this paragraph and the conclusion.

 For further practice, complete the IELTS Supplementary activity on page 120.

Writing

UNIT 11 Writing your answer

Remember that the purpose of the IELTS Writing test is to assess your skill in the following areas:

Task 1	Task 2
interpreting graphs/charts/tables and other graphic information *(Academic)* – writing about facts/trends – comparing and contrasting information OR **engaging in personal correspondence** *(GT)* – explaining a situation – communicating a message	**writing a well-structured argument** – planning carefully – demonstrating a well-organised answer with good paragraphing **presenting a clear point of view** – clarifying main ideas – supporting arguments – giving personal experience/reasons

organising information
– selecting important points/information
– linking statements

writing accurately
– using appropriate structures and vocabulary
– demonstrating good spelling and punctuation

WRITING COHERENTLY

The IELTS exam assesses your ability to write clearly and link your ideas well. On page 121 there is a table which gives a range of linkers and indicates how often they should be used. (Note that it is poor style to repeatedly use certain linkers.) Native speakers frequently use very simple words like *this*, *these/those* and *such* to link ideas together.

- Complete the following sentences by using one of the above words plus a noun:

1 Generally speaking, crime rates in Europe have fallen over the past two years. .... has been the result of new approaches to punishment.

2 Just under 40% of people in the UK and 50% of Americans say that work is the most important part of their lives. .... increase further if we take into account retired people looking back on their working lives.

3 When a group of Australian schoolchildren was interviewed, the majority said they preferred their teachers to be humorous yet kind. However, ... are not as highly rated by teachers.

4 Read the following paragraph and underline any words which help link ideas together.

There is always some controversy over whether it is important to spend large sums of money on medical research or whether more of this money should be directed towards treating patients. Obviously some medical research is essential. Without it, we would have no vaccinations against diseases such as polio, no drugs such as antibiotics and no treatments like x-rays or radiotherapy. Nevertheless, the field of medical research is very competitive and this has financial disadvantages. Take, for example, the current research being conducted on the HIV virus. In this field it is arguable that money is being wasted in that scientists throughout the world are working independently towards the same ultimate goal – to find a cure for AIDS – and with the same hope of becoming famous in the process. Surely it would be more productive and less costly if these scientists joined forces and an international research team was set up with joint international funding.

BUILDING COMPLEX SENTENCES

Credit is given in the IELTS test for the successful control of complex sentence structures. A complex sentence is basically a number of simple sentences linked together using appropriate words and structures. Read the following sets of sentences and see if you can link each set together into one complex sentence.

TEST TIP

It is important to demonstrate your ability to control complex sentences and to link your ideas but don't overdo it! A good piece of writing contains a balance of simple and complex structures and not every sentence has to be linked. Sometimes a short, simple sentence can have a great deal of impact.

5 The graph is about student numbers in the UK.
The number of students in higher education has risen.
The rise has taken place over the last five years.

6 Students were asked how much they expect to earn when they start work.
40 per cent of them expect to earn about £21,000.
2 per cent expect to earn £40,000 or more.

7 A typical police force in Britain has 2500 officers.
A typical town has a population of 180,000.
At any one time, there are only 10 officers patrolling the streets of a typical town.

8 Drink-driving laws vary from country to country.
In Poland it is illegal to drive with more than 20 mg of alcohol in your blood.
In Italy it is illegal to drive with more than 80 mg of alcohol in your blood.

9 The percentage of one-person households in France has risen over the past 10 years.
In 1989, 27 per cent of households in France belonged to single people.
In 1999, 30 per cent of households in France belonged to single people.

10 The enrolment of students in first-degree courses has changed since last year.
The biggest change has taken place in the Biological Sciences.
9 per cent more students have enrolled in the Biological Sciences this year.
55,000 students enrolled in the Biological Sciences this year.

11 Read the following paragraph which describes the results of a survey. There are no grammatical mistakes in the paragraph, but the ideas could be more clearly explained and linked. See whether you can improve it with the help of some of the words and phrases you have learnt so far.

A sample of one hundred people were interviewed at random about their views on the Internet. Most people had heard of the computer facility. Few knew how to use it. 20% of the people had access to it. The people who said they could use the Internet were students or were under 40 years of age. The people who had not heard of it were 60 years old or more. The sample was felt to be representative of the general population.

 For further practice, do the Supplementary activity on page 121.

The Speaking Module

The IELTS Speaking test takes the form of a one-to-one interview. There are three parts to the Speaking test. These allow you to demonstrate your spoken English skills through a number of tasks. The tasks are designed to elicit a range of language on a variety of topics.

The whole interview takes between eleven and fourteen minutes. Here is an overview of the Speaking test format showing the three parts and the approximate timing of each.

	Interaction
Part 1 Introduction and interview 4–5 minutes	The candidate has the opportunity to speak on familiar topics. The examiner asks a number of questions to which the candidate should reply as fully as possible.
Part 2 Individual long turn 3–4 minutes	The candidate is asked to give a short talk for 1–2 minutes on a topic chosen by the examiner. The candidate has a minute to prepare and then speaks on the topic without stopping.
Part 3 Two-way discussion 4–5 minutes	The candidate is presented with more abstract questions broadly linked to the topic introduced in Part 2, and is encouraged to engage in extensive discussion
11–14 minutes	

IELTS Bands	
9	Expert user
8	Very good user
7	Good user
6	Competent user
5	Modest user
4	Limited user
3	Extremely limited user
2	Intermittent user
1	Non-user

THE EXAMINER'S ROLE

IELTS examiners are teachers who have been specially trained to rate spoken English on the IELTS scale. They are chosen to be helpful and encouraging so that you can do your best on the day of the test. They know that you may be nervous but they can only assess what they hear so they will expect you to speak up. The examiners rate your language on a scale of 1–9 in four broad areas. In brief, they want to find out if you can:

- speak fluently and link ideas coherently
- demonstrate a range of appropriate vocabulary
- use accurate grammar and appropriate register
- speak so that you can be understood

THE CANDIDATE'S ROLE

Part 1

The examiner will ask you some questions about yourself and your interests, studies or working life. You should:

- reply by offering a full and appropriate response in each case, taking the initiative where possible.
- always offer more than *yes* or *no* as an answer as your examiner can only rate what he or she hears, and you need to make the very best of this chance to show off your skills.
- use Part 1 to overcome any nerves and demonstrate your basic fluency.

Part 2

The examiner will give you a topic, which is also written on a card, and will hand you some paper and a pencil to make notes. You have a minute to think about what you are going to say. You should:

- think about the topic for a moment and decide how you are going to tackle it.
- use the preparation time wisely by jotting down some key ideas (but do not try to write out a speech).
- make the talk interesting and lively.

Part 3

The examiner will invite you to discuss a number of issues, broadly related in theme to the Part 2 topic. You should:

- try to give informed, interesting and appropriate responses, but remember there is no right or wrong answer.
- use this part of the test to demonstrate your control of language, your ability to express abstract ideas and to support your opinions appropriately.
- show a willingness to provide extended replies.

Speaking

UNIT 1 Part one of the Speaking test – the interview

In Part 1 of the interview the examiner will introduce him or herself to you and ask you your name. You must show some photo identification.

The examiner will then ask you some questions focusing on areas such as your interests, studies or working life. You need to offer interesting responses and to show that you can develop your answers. However, you are not expected to provide a point of view or argue a case.

BECOMING MORE FLUENT

Fluency in speech is the ability to maintain a flow of language without unnatural hesitation and without demanding unreasonable patience of the listener. In other words it is the ability to 'keep going' and includes a number of micro strategies such as willingness to participate and preparedness to respond fully to questions asked by the examiner. Becoming more fluent takes practice, so try using English as often as possible with your friends as well as with English speakers.

- Look at the table below. Take a minute to complete the table by filling in the spaces in each column. You need only enter two or three words in each column.

Home town and family	Hobbies	Favourite food	Languages spoken
	tennis		

- Go round the classroom and speak to as many of your classmates as you can.
- Ask questions based on the table. When you form the questions, you should use the *simple present tense*.
- Report back to the group telling them what you learned about the people you interviewed. Try to make the information flow naturally. For example:

I spoke to Kumiko. She lives in Kyoto and has one brother. Her favourite food is sashimi but she quite likes Australian meat pies. She speaks Japanese fluently of course, and English quite well.

WILLINGNESS TO PARTICIPATE AND EXPAND

- Think of some of the little things that you did over the last weekend.
- Write them down in note form but do not show them to your partner. Try to write at least five activities using the *simple past tense*. For example:

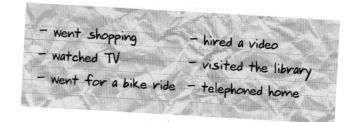

- went shopping
- watched TV
- went for a bike ride
- hired a video
- visited the library
- telephoned home

None of the activities in the list is very unusual. However, all of them lend themselves to E X P A N S I O N.

For each activity you write down, think of a couple of ways in which you could expand the information to make it more interesting to a listener in a conversation. In other words, what additional details can you give? Below is an example of how you could expand on a topic.

I hired a video on Saturday with some friends. It was called .... It's a film about .... It was good/bad/OK because ....

- Look at the list of question words in the box below. Check in the supplementary materials on page 125 if you are uncertain of the grammatical rule for asking WH– questions.

Why?	How much?
When?	How often?
Where?	How good?
What?	How easy?

- Now ask your partner what he or she did at the weekend. As soon as they give you an answer, ask another question using one of the question words above to find out more information. Each time your partner replies, ask another question until you have asked six questions.
- Change roles. Practise your expansion strategy until providing more information to your listener becomes almost automatic!

MORE PRACTICE FOR PART ONE

In Part 1 of the IELTS test you will have to respond by giving full and rounded answers. This means you need to know how to link your ideas.

- Look at the ideas in the picture below.
- Read how the girl links them together to form one cohesive idea. Then say them out loud so that they flow smoothly and sound natural.
- Do the same with the other sets of ideas in the table below. You can use the words supplied in the column on the right or use your own linking words, but limit yourself to two sentences for each set of ideas.
- Now think of a question to which your idea is an appropriate answer.

1	I need to learn English. English is very important. English will help me to get an interesting job. I want to work in the tourism industry.	because, if, which, and
2	I work in a bank. I am a bank teller. Working in a bank can be interesting / boring. Many people do their banking by telephone or on the Internet now.	as, which, but, although
3	Tennis is a wonderful game. To play tennis well you have to be very determined. I enjoy playing tennis. I enjoy watching tennis.	because, but, and, as well as
4	I live in an apartment. The apartment is small. I would like to have a larger place to live. One day I will.	at the moment, which, but, hopefully
5	Take-away food is very popular in many countries. Take-away food is bad for our health. Take-away food is expensive. Cooking at home is more sensible.	even though, because
6	My school was very large. There were hundreds of children at my school. It was impossible to know everyone at the school. I did not know all the teachers.	and, because, even
7	I love movies. I like watching the TV. I don't like live theatre. I don't like opera.	while, but, However, and, either
8	I swim / run to keep fit. Keeping fit is important. People who are not fit run the risk of getting ill. It is difficult to study if you are not well.	because, which, if, unless

- In the interview you may be asked to answer questions on some of the topics below. Choose one of them and be prepared to say something about a number of sub-topics related to the topic you have chosen.

    your family
    your hobbies
    your education
    your home town
    festivals and national holidays

- Write down your topic and sub-topics on a piece of paper and give it to your partner.
- Using the notes as a prompt, ask each other a general question about the main topic, e.g.

Can you tell me about the education system in your country?

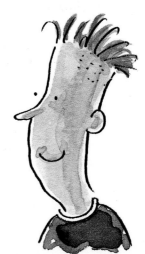

- Then ask specific questions to draw out the information in the notes about the sub-topics. Try to ask questions with WH– words.

Tell me about the different types of schools in your country.

Did you have to wear a school uniform?

What are the benefits of school uniforms?

What exams must students take in your country?

Speaking

In Part 2 of the test you will be asked to give a short talk for one to two minutes on a topic chosen by the examiner. You will have a minute to think about what you are going to say, and to make some notes. Then you will have up to two minutes to speak.
The examiner will remain silent while you are speaking, but may stop you when the time is up by asking you a related follow-up question.
Part 2 offers an opportunity to show the examiner your ability to keep going without unnatural hesitation and to demonstrate your speaking skills including pronunciation.

PREPARING YOUR TALK

- Below is an example of a topic for Part 2. Look at the topic and the three mini questions which accompany it. The Part 2 topic will always follow this format with one main topic and three sub-topics, and will usually focus on a familiar or personal area.

> Describe a place you have lived in that you particularly liked.
>
> You should say:
>
> ♦ when you lived there
> ♦ who you lived with
> ♦ what was most memorable about this place

- First, read the instruction carefully and decide how you are going to approach the topic. In this case you are asked to describe a place where you have lived. If you have only ever lived in one place, then you should describe that place. If you have lived in a number of different places, then you will need to make a quick decision.
- Think about the topic for a moment.
- Underline any key words that strike you as important, e.g. *describe, particularly liked.*

- Decide which place you are going to describe.
- Jot down some key ideas drawing on your own experience. Here is an example.

NOTES

- Perth, Australia – student hall of residence
- 2 years
- other overseas students
- very friendly place, beautiful gardens & sporting facilities
- Sometimes homesick

- Below is a list of possible ways to introduce this topic.
- Practise using them all so that you have a number of different 'openings' for your talk.

I'd like to talk about ....
I've chosen to talk about ....
I'm going to talk about ....
I've lived in quite a few places, but one place I particularly liked was ....
I've really only ever lived in ...., so I'll talk about that.

EXPLAINING HOW YOU FEEL – NOW AND THEN

In the Long Turn you may need to be able to describe how you feel about something now or felt about something in the past. Here are some ways of expressing how you feel. Don't be afraid to express your feelings in this way – it will sound very natural and it also gives **emphasis** to the reason, while allowing the listeners **time** to digest your response.

- The expressions below are all in the present tense. Turn them into past tense expressions so that you can also use them to describe a feeling in the past. The first two have been done as an example.

What I like about Athens is that	you can go to the beach after work.
The reason I don't like London is that	it takes ages to travel from one place to another.
The reason why I enjoy .... is that	you ....
One of the good things about .... is being able	to ....
One of the bad things about .... is not being able	to ....
One of the problems with .... is that	you can't ....

MORE PRACTICE FOR PART TWO

- Look at the Part 2 task below.
- Read it carefully to make sure you fully understand the topic and the sub-topics.

> Describe a job that you would like to do in the future.
>
> You should say:
>
> - why you are attracted to this job
> - how much training, if any, would be necessary
> - what kind of personal qualities it would require

- Think about the topic for a moment.
- Underline any key words that strike you as important.
- Decide on a future job or career that you can talk about.
- Jot down at least two key ideas for each of the sub-topics.

NOTES: future career

-
-
-
-
-
-

- Now work with a partner and give your talk. Speak for at least one minute without stopping.
- For further practice, try recording your talk if this is practical for you. Listen to your own talk again and make a note of any grammar problems you had or pronunciation difficulties.

GIVING SHORT ANSWERS TO THE FOLLOW-UP QUESTIONS

After you have given your talk, the examiner may ask you one or two related follow-up questions which you should answer briefly. The follow-up question will probably only require a *yes* or *no* answer and a couple of other words.

We often give short answers in English by simply repeating the auxiliary verb or the verb *to be* or *to do* which was used in the question. You must use the same tense as the question. Here is an example of a follow-up question to the task above with appropriate short answers.

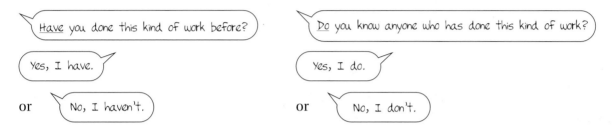

Have you done this kind of work before?

Yes, I have.

or   No, I haven't.

Do you know anyone who has done this kind of work?

Yes, I do.

or   No, I don't.

- Look at the questions below.
- Underline the verbs which you are going to use in your short answers.
- Now give the short answers using *yes* **and** *no* to these questions.

   1 Were there any things you didn't like about this place where you lived?

   2 Is it easy to get work in this field?

   3 Are you interested in this kind of work?

   4 Did you read about this course in the newspaper?

   5 Had you studied English before you came here?

   6 Will you go to university after this course?

   7 Can you speak more than one foreign language?

   8 Are you going to study in America?

If you don't want to sound too direct, you can often include the words *I think* after the *yes* or *I don't think* after the *no*, but you must still include your short answer verb. Alternatively you can use the short answers *I think so* or *I don't think so*. Here is an example:

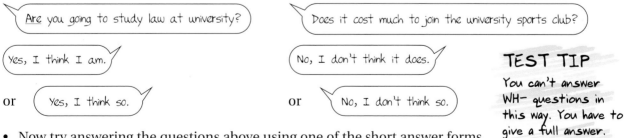

Are you going to study law at university?

Yes, I think I am.

or   Yes, I think so.

Does it cost much to join the university sports club?

No, I don't think it does.

or   No, I don't think so.

TEST TIP

You can't answer WH– questions in this way. You have to give a full answer.

- Now try answering the questions above using one of the short answer forms.

Speaking

In Part 3 you will be presented with some more abstract questions. These will be broadly linked to the topic introduced in Part 2. You will have to take part in a discussion with the examiner.

This is your opportunity to show off your vocabulary as well as your ability to express an opinion and justify your ideas. Your language needs to be accurate as well as appropriate to the situation, i.e. a formal discussion. However, don't be afraid to say what you think. You will not be marked for your opinion. Try to back your opinions with reasons. Your examiner will welcome your views.

EXPLORING THE THEME

After you have given your talk, the examiner will invite you to explore the topic further. The examiner will choose a number of themes and ask questions related to each theme.

In the last unit we looked at ways of preparing a talk on the topic *A place where you once lived.*

- The questions on page 107 are all linked broadly to the topic of housing and the way we live. They can be divided into the three sub-themes of:
    Work and Housing
    Architecture
    Housing and the State
- Read the questions on page 107 and underline the words which provide a link to the original topic (*A place where you once lived*).
- Decide which of the three sub-topics the questions belong to. The first one has been done for you.

1 Is it a good idea for people to work from home?

Links to the sub-theme – Work and Housing

2 Would you prefer to live in a house or an apartment?

3 What are the disadvantages of commuting long distances to work?

4 Should the State provide cheap housing for low-income earners?

5 Do you think architects pay more attention to the appearance of buildings than to the basic requirement of shelter?

6 What can be done to help people who are homeless?

7 To what extent does climate determine the kind of houses we build?

PRODUCING A REASONED RESPONSE

- Imagine your examiner has asked you this question. You will need to provide a reasoned and appropriate response.

Should the State provide cheap housing for low-income earners?

- Here is a strategy for approaching a question of this type. If possible, work through these steps with a partner.

1 Re-phrase the question (in your head) in your own words. This will help you to explore the issues raised in the question.
E.g. Is it the responsibility of the government to provide homes for poor people?

2 Decide whether any of the key words raise new questions. E.g. How do we define 'poor'? What kind of things should government be responsible for?

3 Do you have any real views on this question? What are they?

4 Make sure you can give two good reasons to back your opinion.
E.g. Everyone has the right to a place to live. It is the role of a government to provide shelter for people.

5 Begin your answer with the words *I think* or *I don't think*.

See page 123 for other suitable opening expressions and for a sample answer to question 7.

- Here are two examples of a possible response. Underline the words which:
  - introduce an opinion
  - provide evidence or backing for that opinion
- Try reading them out loud to make them come alive.

'Well, yes, I do. I think that the government or the State should provide cheap housing for people who don't earn very much money. Because if we don't do this, they may end up sleeping in the street or in the park, and this will only reflect very badly on our society as a whole.'

'I feel it's really the responsibility of the government to provide housing, just as they should provide education and, ideally, health services. That's one of the reasons why we pay our taxes.'

MORE PRACTICE FOR PART 3

In Unit 2 you practised giving a talk about a job you would like to do. Following on from this topic, the Part 3 discussion could centre on the theme of employment.

- Look at the questions below which are based on the theme of employment.
- Try to think of some more questions that you could ask in order to explore the topic of employment. (Refer to page 124 for help with forming questions.)

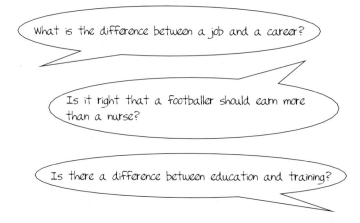

What is the difference between a job and a career?

Is it right that a footballer should earn more than a nurse?

Is there a difference between education and training?

- Write each of your questions on a separate piece of paper and put them all in a hat with the three questions above.
- Each person should draw one question and try to give a reasoned answer on the spot to the rest of the class. Make sure your answer relates back to the topic.
- As you listen to each other's answers, make notes and be prepared to ask at least one question after each person has answered.

Remember! When you get to university you will regularly be expected to join in discussions in your tutorial groups, so this is a good place to start.

 For further practice, do the Supplementary activity on page 126.

Supplementary Activities

LISTENING UNIT 1

- Go back to the pictures on page 8 and the words you wrote in the balloons. Choose one of the situations and write a short dialogue, expanding on what you wrote before.

- Read the dialogue out loud to your classmates and see if they can name the speakers. Make sure you include words that will highlight *who* the speakers are, *where* they are and *why* they are speaking.

- Try writing another dialogue for a new situation not shown here.

- Act out the new dialogue to the class. The rest of the class must guess the context and roles of the speakers from the dialogue.

LISTENING UNIT 2

- Choose a situation from the list below.

Ringing a friend about a dinner arrangement that you need to change	Ringing some friends to invite them to dinner at home	Inviting an overseas visitor to join you for dinner at a restaurant	Enquiring about the availability of a table in a restaurant

- Imagine that you need to make this telephone call, but when you get through, you find that you have to leave a short message on an answering machine.

- Work out what you will say in your message. Remember to keep the message short and include only the important details.

- Don't forget to include your name and contact telephone number if you don't know the person.

- Read your message to your partner. Can they say which situation it relates to?

LISTENING UNIT 3

- Think of an everyday object. Work out how to describe it without using its name or saying what it is used for.

- Practise describing the object with your partner.

- The class divides into two teams, making sure that the pairs remain together.

- Each person describes their object in front of the class.

- To gain a point, the other team must be able to identify your object.

LISTENING UNIT 4

Follow-up to Unit 4, Extract 2

- Write a paragraph to sum up the main ideas of the talk on stamp design. If necessary, go back and listen to the talk again, making notes of the main ideas. Do not include any examples or supporting detail in your summary.

- Read some of the summaries out to the class. Did you agree on what the main ideas of the talk were?

LISTENING UNIT 5

Follow-up to Unit 5, Extract 2

- Look at the following expressions which occurred in the conversation. Try to work out their meaning with your partner. How many of them can be interpreted literally?

  – I beg your pardon!   – pushing back the frontiers of science

  – Oh, Frank, you know what I mean!   – to get away from it all

  – from the cradle to the grave – to have a roof over their heads

  – the party's over

- Can you remember which speaker used which expression? If not, listen again. Make sure you know exactly what each expression means in the context of this conversation.

LISTENING UNIT 6

- Look at the recording script for Unit 6, Extract 2. Write five new questions based on the script. The answers should be no more than three words. Give the questions to your partner.

- Now close the book and listen to the extract once more without looking at the script. Try to answer your partner's questions.

LISTENING UNIT 7

- Listen to the lecture on child language acquisition again (Unit 7, Extract 2).

- Make a note of all the 'signpost words' that you hear. Compare your list with your partner.

- Look at the recording script. The signpost words have been written in bold. Do you agree with them all? Did you find any others?

- Now write a summary of the lecture in 150 words.

READING UNIT 1

Exercise A

• Look at the titles, sub-headings and opening paragraphs of some of the articles in a newspaper or magazine.

• Pick some that you think are helpful to the reader and some that are not.

• Cut out the complete articles and take them into class.

• Discuss the articles as a group, by referring to the orientation questions in this unit.

• Can you improve on any of the titles/sub-headings?

Exercise B

• Pick an article from a journal or magazine that you think has a good introduction.

• Cut off the title, sub-heading and first paragraph.

• Exchange these with a partner.

• Discuss what you would expect to read about in your partner's article.

• Read the whole of your partner's article when you have finished your discussions.

READING UNIT 2

• Find an article in a newspaper or magazine that contains a lot of factual information.

• Write five questions on the article.

• Check with your teacher that you have chosen the right sort of information to test and make sure that the questions can be answered using three words or less.

• Exchange your passage and questions with someone else.

READING UNIT 3

IELTS Reading

*Using **NO MORE THAN THREE WORDS**, complete the following sentences using words from the reading passage 'Salty rice plant boosts harvests' on page 40.*

Write your answers in boxes 14–18 on your answer sheet.

Some farms have been ...(14)... because the soil is too salty.

The research team hope to assist in the adaptation of other ...(15)... to salt water.

…(16)… of farmland is ruined annually.

The team aims to develop rice plants that …(17)… excess salt.

The team must wait for …(18)… before they know whether they have been successful.

READING UNIT 4

Exercise A

- Select an interesting article from a magazine or newspaper that has five or six paragraphs with clear ideas/topics/themes in each paragraph.

- Write some headings for these.

- Jumble up your headings.

- Exchange articles with another pair of students. See if you can match the headings to the paragraphs.

- Discuss how difficult or easy it was. Would you have written the same headings?

Exercise B

- Select an interesting article from a magazine or newspaper that has five or six paragraphs with clear ideas/topics/themes in each paragraph.

- Cut up the article into separate paragraphs and jumble the pieces of paper up.

- Exchange these with another pair of students and see if you can put their article together again. How easy or difficult was it? Why do you think this was?

READING UNIT 5

IELTS Reading

The Reading Passage 'Prehistoric Insects Spawn New Drugs' on pages 46–7 has six paragraphs labelled A–F. Which paragraphs contain the following information?

Write the appropriate letters A–F in boxes 9–13 on your answer sheet.

NB *You only need ONE letter for each answer.*
You may use any letter more than once.

9 two examples of bacteria that can now resist antibiotic drugs

10 the length of time we have been using antibiotics

11 the original source of the new drugs being discussed

12 the scientist responsible for setting up the research into fossilised insects

13 examples of other similar studies that have been undertaken

READING UNIT 6

- Read the following excerpts from articles. Discuss what is being said in each one and then write a short, one-sentence summary of the views or arguments being put forward.

16 Copyright is a treasure for the pedant. It is also doomed, according to some who should know. It is, of course, computers which pose a serious threat to the very notion of copyright. The problem is bad enough for authors of computer programs, which can be copied in a few minutes. How many computer users reading this can honestly say that every program they use is fully paid for? It's about to get very much worse, and seriously to affect those of us who produce human-readable prose.

17 Scientists have scant idea of why we sleep, and find dreaming an even bigger mystery. Theories range from the brain clearing its memory of junk to the liberation of suppressed subconscious urges. The reason for their ignorance lies in the astonishing design of the brain. The most complex known object in the universe, it contains as many nerve cells – neurons – as there are stars in the Milky Way; about 100 billion of them. Each communicates with thousands of its neighbours, generating an unimaginable chatter.

18 Sustainability in the use of soils does not mean avoiding all changes, or trying to restore damaged soils to some pristine state. But it implies that human activities ought not to deplete resources of soil at a faster rate than these can be replenished by natural processes or human intervention. We must be careful not to cause lasting damage to the natural resilience of soils, about which we have little understanding.

READING UNIT 7

IELTS Reading

*Complete the summary of the Reading Passage 'Books, Films and Plays' on pages 53–4. Choose **NO MORE THAN THREE** words from the passage for each Question 14–20.*

BOOKS, FILMS and PLAYS

Example   *Answer*

The novel is arguably the most versatile artistic ... **(0)** ...   *medium*

But the artistic freedom this brings with it can cause ... **(14)** ... Unlike other writers, ... **(15)** ... can expect his or her work to be accepted with few, if any, alterations because the work represents one ... **(16)** ... only. Films and screenplays on the other hand, may have to undergo ... **(17)** ... to suit everyone involved. In fact, screenplay writers can find that they eventually lose ... **(18)** ... their work. Writers of plays are a little more fortunate in that they are given the ... **(19)** ... to decide who directs and acts in their play, but film and TV writers often pass all responsibility for the final product to ... **(20)** ... .

READING UNIT 8

- Get into small groups and select one of the following topics/themes:

  English language courses   Jobs   Travel   Books/films   Restaurants

- Cut out some advertisements from magazines or newspapers on your chosen topic/theme.

- Take them to class and discuss them in your group. Pick the six that have the most factual information in them and paste them onto an A4 page.

- See if you can write some matching questions on your set.

- Exchange sets and questions with another group and see if you can successfully do the matching exercise.

- Discuss which set worked best as a class.

READING UNIT 9

IELTS Reading

The Reading passage on page 63 has advertisements for student accommodation. Which residence offers the following?

Write the appropriate name in boxes 15–19 on your answer sheet.

NB *You only need **ONE** name for each answer.*
You may use any name more than once.

15   views of the countryside

16   immediate bookings

17   help in finding a room-mate

18   a set of ground rules

19   young management

WRITING UNIT 1

Exercise A

- The graph below shows the percentage of teachers in a school who read the newspaper on each day of the week. Describe some of the facts illustrated in the graph using the structures you have learnt so far.

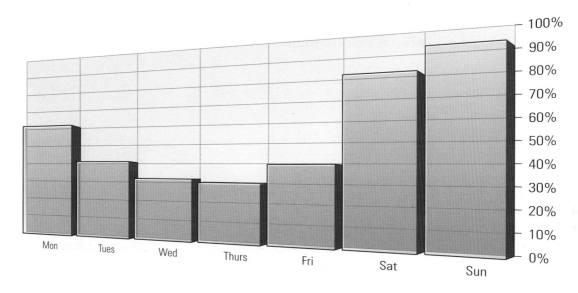

Exercise B

- Draw a pie chart to show what percentage of your time you spend on the following activities each week:

  cleaning   shopping   entertainment

  watching TV   studies   sport

- Write some sentences that describe the chart. Try to organise the information appropriately and join your sentences with *and, but, while, although* or use *as … as.*

- Cover up your pie charts and exchange your descriptions. Your partner must try to draw your pie chart from your description and you must try to draw your partner's pie chart from his or her description.

WRITING UNIT 2

Exercise A

- Find some graphs or charts and bring them to class.

- Discuss all the information on the axes or labels.

- Select one or two and describe the trends they show.

Exercise B

You should spend about 20 minutes on this task.

> *The graphs below show amounts of fish caught in the three largest oceans and who the main consumers are.*
>
> *Describe the information shown in the graphs.*
>
> You should write at least 150 words.

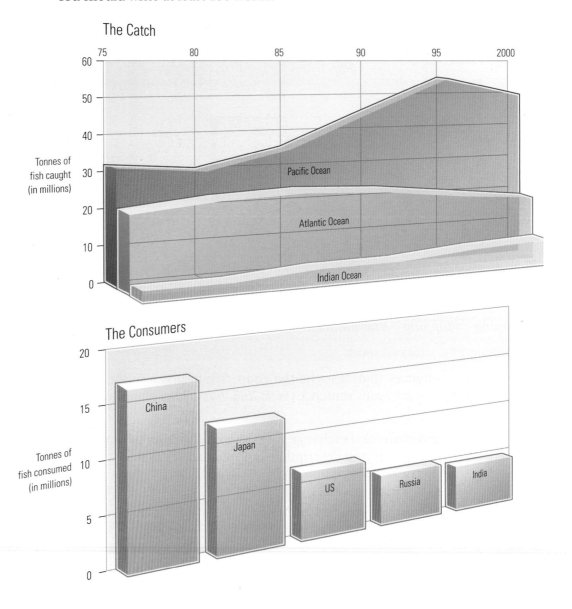

WRITING UNIT 3

IELTS Writing   **Task 1**

You should spend about 20 minutes on this task.

> *The table and graph below give information about the amount of money in US$ billions spent on advertising in Europe.*
>
> *Describe the information shown.*

You should write at least 150 words.

European Advertising Spending 1996–9 (*US $ billions*)				
	Germany	UK	France	Spain
1996	16	14	9	3
1997	17	15	10	3
1998	23	17	11	4
1999	25	19	12	5

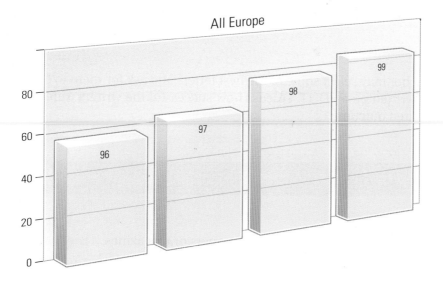

All Europe

WRITING UNIT 4

- Draw a diagram of a simple, everyday process (such as doing up a tie) using as few words as possible.

- Copy your diagram onto an overhead transparency and describe the process it shows to the class.

- Select one of the diagrams and write a description of it.

WRITING UNITS 5 AND 6

Part 1

- Think of a situation (either real or imaginary) that caused you a problem and that you could write a letter to someone about.

- Decide how you felt about the situation and what the purpose of your letter is going to be *before* you write it.

- Write your letter either at home or in class. Write about 150 words. Do not sign the letter.

Part 2

- Fold your letter up and put it into a pile with all the other letters that your classmates have written. Jumble the letters up.

- Pick a letter from the pile, open it up and read it.

- Consider how the letter has been written and what sort of reply it merits. Write an appropriate reply in 20 minutes.

- Find out who wrote the original letter and show them your reply.

Part 3

- Your teacher may select some of the best letters and ask for them to be read out in class or written on an OHT. Discuss how successful the writers were in achieving their desired outcome.

WRITING UNIT 7

Part 1

- Cut out some letters' pages from newspapers or magazines.

- In pairs, select a topic that is interesting and that people can debate.

- Write a statement 'for' or 'against' the topic on a small piece of paper.

- Fold up the piece of paper and put it in a hat or box.

Part 2

- Take a piece of folded paper out of the hat or box.

- Read the sentence and discuss as a class the sort of areas that could be covered in a written discussion of the topic.

- Suggest how you might develop ideas on the topic.

WRITING UNIT 8

- Discuss the techniques used by the following writers in their introductory paragraphs. How do you expect these writers to continue their responses?

i
My response to this argument depends on what is meant by a 'company'. There is surely a difference between a small family-run business and an international firm with hundreds of employees and a well-established hierarchical structure. I intend to illustrate how some of these differences are significant to the argument put forward.

ii
I certainly believe that employees should be made to feel that they make a positive contribution to the running of their company. High self-esteem amongst staff is definitely important. However, whilst I agree that this type of managerial approach will have internal benefits, I am less convinced that it will increase a company's profits.

WRITING UNIT 9

- Complete the paragraph below by using an appropriate word or structure for each gap.

One of the main arguments (3) _____ school uniforms is that they make all schoolchildren within the same school look the same. (4) _____ they cover up any obvious socio-economic differences and thus prevent children from feeling embarrassed about the clothes they wear. (5) _____ this is a very important consideration. Children should be free to concentrate on their studies rather than worrying about their appearance. (6) _____ it is not ideal to take away people's freedom of choice by imposing a uniform but I (7) _____ that children have any feelings about such things. Neither do I (8) _____ uniforms pose a financial burden on families. (9) _____ they would have to spend some money on whatever their children wear to school and uniforms, in particular, are usually relatively cheap to buy.

- Compare your answers and discuss them.

WRITING UNIT 10

Academic Module

IELTS Writing	Task 2

You should spend about 40 minutes on this task.

Present a written argument or case to an educated reader with no specialist knowledge of the following topic:

> *As more and more students enter universities, academic qualifications are becoming devalued. To get ahead in many professions, more than one degree is now required and in future it is likely that people will take a number of degree courses before even starting work. This is an undesirable situation.*
>
> *Do you agree or disagree?*

You should write at least 250 words.

You should use your own ideas, knowledge and experience and support your arguments with examples and relevant evidence.

General Training module

IELTS Writing	Task 2

You should spend about 40 minutes on this task.

As part of a class assignment you have to write about the following topic:

> *Disruptive school students have a negative influence on others. Students who are noisy and disobedient should be grouped together and taught separately.*
>
> *Do you agree or disagree?*
>
> *Give reasons for your answer*

You should write at least 250 words.

A model answer, one of many possible approaches, is given on page 186.

WRITING UNIT 11

Use the following words to help you to link your ideas together.

Use sparingly	Use moderately	Use as desired
first, second, etc.	while/meanwhile	such
moreover	whereas	this/these
furthermore	although	those
in addition	inspite of / despite	and
nevertheless/nonetheless	even though	but
on the one/other hand	as a result	also
besides	however	yet
consequently	since	even
likewise	similarly	or
conversely	thus	so
in contrast/comparison	in turn	for

- Link the ideas below into a coherent paragraph.

Why is relaxation important? There are several arguments.
a) Life is much faster than it used to be e.g. modes of travel, technology. The body can't keep up.
b) (possibly more important) Enthusiasm for work is renewed after a break. Mistakes/accidents are less likely. We have new ideas/approaches. Everyone benefits. Do some people need more relaxation than others? The more we have, the more we want? I think so. Age/health/stress/finances etc. play a part but individuals differ. So must keep a balance. Take holidays and breaks but not too many.

SPEAKING UNIT 1

- Take a minute to complete a diagrammatic picture of your family, showing your relatives. We call this a family tree. You don't have to include everyone in your family, but be prepared to describe the people you include, saying where they live and what they are like. Then hand your family tree to your partner.

- Look at your partner's family tree and ask each other for information about some of the people included. Try to give two pieces of information about each person. Use language like this:

  A: I see you have two brothers. Can you tell me something about them?
  B: One of them/The older one is living in America and the other is still at home. *or* My older brother is studying at university. The younger one is still at school.

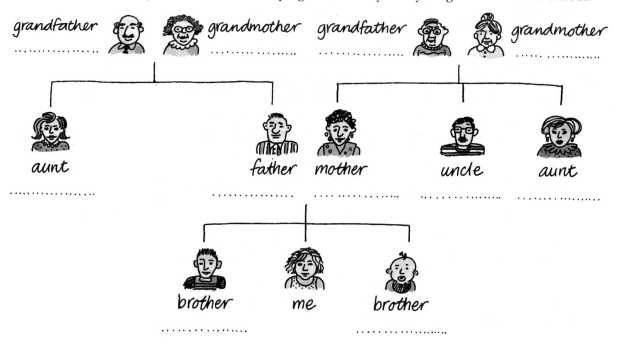

SPEAKING UNIT 2 – FURTHER PRACTICE FOR PART TWO

Here is another example of a Part 2 task.

Describe your ideal study room.

You should say:

◆ where it would be
◆ what equipment and furniture it would contain
◆ how it would be decorated

Possible follow-up questions are:

Do you think you will ever find somewhere like this?
Do you think your surroundings matter when you are studying?

TALKING ABOUT EMPLOYMENT – FURTHER PRACTICE FOR PART 2

- Look at the list of professions below. What kind of person would be suited to do each of these jobs? Are the qualities required necessarily positive?

economist	accountant	translator	advertising executive
surgeon	teacher	lawyer	computer programmer
airline pilot	nurse	policeman	company director
journalist	actor	secretary	vet
politician	interpreter	engineer	musician

- Choose one of the jobs listed above.
- Prepare a one-minute talk to give to the class on what kind of person you feel would be suited to that job and why.
- Make notes for your talk, but do not write it out word for word and do not read your talk. You may like to use the board to help illustrate the ideas using the main points as prompts to guide you. It may help to divide the ideas into educational requirements and personal qualities. Here are some expressions to help you make your points.

I think …	… a pilot needs to be able to think quickly.
I believe …	… nursing is a profession for dedicated people.
As far as I can see …	… one requirement for being a politician is having a very thick skin.
I would say that …	… good computer programmers are usually good mathematicians.
I would think that …	… a lawyer needs to be a fast reader.

- As you listen to each other's talks, make notes and be prepared to ask at least one question after each person has completed his or her talk.

- For further practice, try recording your talk, if this is practical for you. Listen to your own talk again and make a note of any grammar problems you had or pronunciation difficulties.

FURTHER PRACTICE FOR PART 3

> To what extent does climate determine the kind of houses we build?

- Here is an example of a possible response. Underline the words which:
  - introduce an opinion
  - provide evidence or backing for that opinion.

> Well, in my view climate probably has quite a lot to do with the way we design and build our houses. For instance, in countries where it snows a lot, you find houses built with a steep roof … so that the snow can't settle on the roof, and … you know … damage the roof. But in warm climates the houses are often built with a verandah to keep the sun out of the rooms and to provide a cool place to sit.

Guidelines for forming questions in English

1 Inversion of subject and verb	Main verb + subject
In this case the main verb must be a modal auxiliary verb, e.g. *can/ must/ will/ would* or the verb *to be* (all tenses) or the verb *to have* used as an auxiliary to form the present perfect. The subject can be either a pronoun, a noun or proper noun, a gerund or a name. This type of question is usually spoken with downward intonation.	**Can** Joseph swim? **Is** the baby asleep? **Were** you born in New York? **Are** your friends coming to the party? **Has** anyone seen my pen?

2 Making questions using Do	Do + subject + verb + object
Do is used with all verbs which are not auxiliaries. Invert the subject and the verb *Do* and add the simple infinitive form of the verb which carries the message. Remember to change the form of *Do* to fit the person and the tense. Negative questions with *Don't* indicate surprise. This type of question is usually spoken with falling intonation.	**Do you** like ice cream? **Does Mary** speak Japanese? **Did your brother** study at university? **Don't you** want to learn English? **Didn't he** receive the information?

3 Making questions using Wh- question words + do				
In this case the *Wh-* question word comes at the beginning of the sentence but is *not* the subject of the verb *do*.	**Where** **What** **When** **Why** **Who(m)** **How** **Which**	**do/does** **did**	pronoun or noun as subject of DO verb	verb
Examples	**Where**	**do**	you	live?
	What	**did**	the students	see at the cinema?

4 Making questions using Wh- question words without do			
In this case the *Wh-* question word comes at the beginning of the sentence and is used as the subject.	**Who** **What** **Which** as subject of verb	verb	object or complement
Example	**Who** **What** **Which (way)**	likes is is	chicken with rice? that noise? correct?

5 Making questions with question tags
Although this is a very common way of asking questions in English, we usually only use question tags to confirm something we already know, or, in some cases, to suggest surprise or irritation.

6 Using intonation to form questions
Although you may hear people asking questions simply by raising their voice at the end of the sentence, this is not always regarded as adequate or appropriate. Rising intonation is common when asking questions but often indicates that you are asking for clarification rather than new information.

SPEAKING UNIT 3

Extending a conversation

- Look at the bubble diagram below on what is important in a job.

- Take a moment to think about each of the issues shown here.

- Be prepared to make a useful comment about each of the issues. Make sure you have an opinion on all the ideas.

- *Preparation: Make up a set of 8 cards based on the 8 ideas in the bubble diagram below. Place a set of the cards face down on the table for each group. Each student picks a card and must talk about the topic for 45 seconds. Replace the card on the bottom of the pile.*

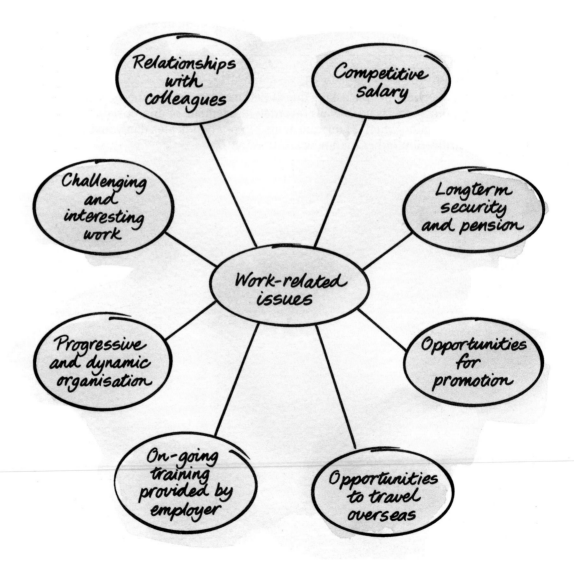

Practice Test

SECTION 1   *Questions 1–10*

Questions 1–2

Circle the appropriate letter.

Example What type of accommodation does the student want?

A

B

C

1 How does he want to travel to the university?

A

B

C

2 How did he feel about living at the hall of residence?

A

B

C

127

Questions 3–6

*Complete the table below using **NO MORE THAN THREE WORDS.***

Property	Advantage	Disadvantage
Two-bedroom house	Near the university	(3) ....
Three-bedroom flat	Near the university	(4) ....
Three-bedroom house	(5)	Far from the university

Address: **(6)** .... , Botany

Questions 7–8

*Circle **TWO** letters.*

Which **TWO** of the following does the agent say are included?

A kitchen cupboards
B garden table
C double bed
D dishwasher
E washing machine
F refrigerator

Questions 9–10

What **TWO** things does the student request before moving in?

A new kitchen cooker
B garden cleared
C back door painted
D carpets cleaned
E windows repaired
F new refrigerator

SECTION 2   Questions 11–20

Questions 11–14

Complete the notes as you listen. Use **NO MORE THAN THREE WORDS** for each answer.

NOTES

Example

Ginger is related to the ___Bamboo___ family.

The Chinese used ginger principally for (11) ....

Ginger was first grown in (12) .... and ....

Spice traders were able to get (13) .... for ginger.

Ginger was introduced to Australia in the (14) .... century.

Questions 15–17

Complete the table below. Use **NO MORE THAN THREE WORDS** for each answer.

Cause	Effect
High rainfall in Queensland	(15) .... for growing ginger
(16) High	Australian ginger was not price competitive
(17)	Supplies of ginger ran low

Questions 18–20

*Complete the fact sheet below. Use **NO MORE THAN THREE WORDS** for each answer.*

BUDERIM COOPERATIVE

FACT SHEET

Cooperative was formed with **(18)** £..

two wooden vats and **(19)** .... of raw ginger.

40% of ginger	**(20)** ....
60% of ginger	exported to Asia, Europe and elsewhere

SECTION 3   *Questions 21–30*

Questions 21–25

*Complete the sentences below. Use **NO MORE THAN THREE WORDS** for each answer.*

According to Dr Clarke:

21   Scientists want to know whether global warming is caused by ....
....

22   Insulation may cause the Earth to
....

23   There are many .... on the global climate.

24   The .... does not remain static.

25   We cannot understand the global climate without understanding ....
....

Questions 26–27

*Complete the table. Use **NO MORE THAN THREE WORDS** for each answer.*

Methods used to measure temperature	Location of instruments
a) From thermometers in buoys	sea
b) When water is drawn through the **(26)** .... of ships	
c) ATSR (infra-red detector)	**(27)** ....

Questions 28–30

*Which **THREE** advantages of the ATSR are mentioned by Dr Clarke? Circle the three correct letters.*

List of Advantages

A   lasts two and a half years
B   measures very accurately
C   produces large amounts of data
D   is located in two places
E   can view 500 kilometres at a time
F   correct to within 3 degrees centigrade

SECTION 4   Questions 31–40

Questions 31–40

Complete the notes below. Write **NO MORE THAN THREE WORDS** for each answer.

JERSEY ZOO

Conservation Course and Wildlife Preservation Trust

Participants:	Students from (31) ....
	Jousseff's area of interest (32) ....
	Jousseff liked to visit the (33) ....
Selection criteria:	Must work with (34) ....
	They have to learn (35) ....
	and (36) ....

Intensive training programme

Theory:	conservation biology
Practice:	work with (37) ....
	to learn animal care

Graduates

Number to date: (38) .... including a former

(39) .... who is in charge of

captive breeding and conservation in his country and a

Mauritian student who is (40) ....

for her country

READING (Academic Module)

READING PASSAGE 1

*You should spend about 20 minutes on **Questions 1–13** which are based on Reading Passage 1 below.*

Creating Artificial Reefs

In the coastal waters of the US, a nation's leftovers have been discarded. Derelict ships, concrete blocks, scrapped cars, army tanks, tyres filled with concrete and redundant planes litter the sea floor. However, this is not waste disposal, but part of a coordinated, state-run programme. To recently arrived fish, plants and other sea organisms, these artificial reefs are an ideal home, offering food and shelter.

Sea-dumping incites widespread condemnation. Little surprise when oceans are seen as 'convenient' dumping grounds for the rubbish we have created but would rather forget. However, scientific evidence suggests that if we dump the right things, sea life can actually be enhanced. And more recently, purpose-built structures of steel or concrete have been employed – some the size of small apartment blocks – principally to increase fish harvests.

The choice of design and materials for an artificial reef depends on where it is going to be placed. In areas of strong currents, for example, a solid concrete structure will be more appropriate than ballasted tyres. It also depends on what species are to be attracted. It is pointless creating high-rise structures for fish that prefer flat or low-relief habitat. But the most important consideration is the purpose of the reef.

In the US, where there is a national reef plan using cleaned up rigs and tanks, artificial reefs have mainly been used to attract fish for recreational fishing or sport-diving. But there are many other ways in which they can be used to manage the marine habitat. For as well as protecting existing habitat, providing purpose-built accommodation for commercial species (such as lobsters and octupi) and acting as sea defences, they can be an effective way of improving fish harvests.

Japan, for example, has created vast areas of artificial habitat – rather than isolated reefs – to increase its fish stocks. In fact, the cultural and historical importance of seafood in Japan is reflected by the fact that it is a world leader in reef technology; what's more, those who construct and deploy reefs have sole rights to the harvest.

In Europe, artificial reefs have been mainly employed to protect habitat. Particularly so in the Mediterranean where reefs have been sunk as physical obstacles to stop illegal trawling, which is destroying sea grass beds and the marine life that depends on them. 'If you want to protect areas of the seabed, you need something that will stop trawlers dead in their tracks,' says Dr Antony Jensen of the Southampton Oceanography Centre.

Italy boasts considerable artificial reef activity. It deployed its first scientifically planned reef using concrete cubes assembled in pyramid forms in 1974 to enhance fisheries and stop trawling. And Spain has built nearly 50 reefs in its waters, mainly to discourage trawling and enhance the productivity of fisheries. Meanwhile, Britain established its first quarried rock artificial reef in 1984 off the Scottish coast, to assess its potential for attracting commercial species.

But while the scientific study of these structures is a little over a quarter of a century old, artificial reefs made out of readily available materials such as bamboo and coconuts have been used by fishermen for centuries. And the benefits have been enormous. By placing reefs close to home, fishermen can save time and fuel. But unless they are carefully managed, these areas can become over-fished. In the Philippines, for example, where artificial reef programmes have been instigated in response to declining fish populations, catches are often allowed to exceed the maximum potential new production of the artificial reef because there is no proper management control.

There is no doubt that artificial reefs have lots to offer. And while purpose-built structures are effective, the real challenge now is to develop environmentally safe ways of using recycled waste to increase marine diversity. This will require more scientific research. For example, the leachates from one of the most commonly used reef materials, tyres, could potentially be harmful to the creatures and plants that they are supposed to attract. Yet few extensive studies have been undertaken into the long-term effects of disposing of tyres at sea. And at the moment, there is little consensus about what is environmentally acceptable to dump at sea, especially when it comes to oil and gas rigs. Clearly, the challenge is

to develop environmentally acceptable ways of disposing of our rubbish while enhancing marine life too. What we must never be allowed to do is have an excuse for dumping anything we like at sea.

Questions 1–3

*The list below gives some of the factors that must be taken into account when deciding how to construct an artificial reef. Which **THREE** of these factors are mentioned by the writer of the article? Write the appropriate letters **A–F** in boxes 1–3 on your answer sheet.*

A   The fishing activity in the area

B   The intended location of the reef

C   The existing reef structures

D   The type of marine life being targeted

E   The function of the reef

F   The cultural importance of the area

Questions 4–8

*Complete the table below. Choose **NO MORE THAN THREE WORDS** from the passage for each answer. Write your answers in boxes 4-8 on your answer sheet.*

Area/country	Type of Reef	Purpose
US	made using old ... (4) ...	to attract fish for leisure activities
Japan	forms large area of artificial habitat	to improve ... (5) ...
Europe	lies deep down to form ... (6) ...	to act as a sea defence
Italy	consists of pyramid shapes made of ... (7) ...	to prevent trawling
Britain	made of rock	to encourage ... (8) ... fish species

Questions 9–12

*Using **NO MORE THAN THREE WORDS**, complete the following sentences. Write your answers in boxes **9–12** on your answer sheet.*

In ... (9) ..., people who build reefs are legally entitled to all the fish they attract.

Trawling inhibits the development of marine life because it damages the ... (10) ... .

In the past, both ... (11) ... were used to make reefs.

To ensure that reefs are not over-fished, good ... (12) ... is required.

Question 13

*Choose the appropriate letter **A–D** and write it in box 13 on your answer sheet.*

13 According to the writer, the next step in the creation of artificial reefs is
   A to produce an international agreement.
   B to expand their use in the marine environment.
   C to examine their dangers to marine life.
   D to improve on purpose-built structures.

READING PASSAGE 2

*You should spend about 20 minutes on **Questions 14–27** which are based on Reading Passage 2 on the following pages.*

Questions 14–19

*Reading Passage 2 has eight paragraphs (**A–H**). Choose the most suitable heading for each paragraph from the list of headings below. Write the appropriate numbers (**i–xi**) in boxes 14–19 on your answer sheet.*

NB *There are more headings than paragraphs so you will not use all of them. You may use any heading more than once.*

List of Headings

i	Gathering the information
ii	Cigarettes produced to match an image
iii	Financial outlay on marketing
iv	The first advertising methods
v	Pressure causes a drop in sales
vi	Changing attitudes allow new marketing tactics
vii	Background to the research
viii	A public uproar is avoided
ix	The innovative move to written adverts
x	A century of uninhibited smoking
xi	Conclusions of the research

---

14 Paragraph A

15 Paragraph B

16 Paragraph C

Example	*Answer*
Paragraph D	iv

17 Paragraph E

18 Paragraph F

19 Paragraph G

Example	*Answer*
Paragraph H	xi

Looking for a Market among Adolescents

A   In 1992, the most recent year for which data are available, the US tobacco industry spent $5 billion on domestic marketing. That figure represents a huge increase from the approximate £250-million budget in 1971, when tobacco advertising was banned from television and radio. The current expenditure translates to about $75 for every adult smoker, or to $4,500 for every adolescent who became a smoker that year. This apparently high cost to attract a new smoker is very likely recouped over the average 25 years that this teen will smoke.

B   In the first half of this century, leaders of the tobacco companies boasted that innovative mass-marketing strategies built the industry. Recently, however, the tobacco business has maintained that its advertising is geared to draw established smokers to particular brands. But public health advocates insist that such advertising plays a role in generating new demand, with adolescents being the primary target. To explore the issue, we examined several marketing campaigns undertaken over the years and correlated them with the ages smokers say they began their habit. We find that, historically, there is considerable evidence that such campaigns led to an increase in cigarette smoking among adolescents of the targeted group.

C   National surveys collected the ages at which people started smoking. The 1955 Current Population Survey (CPS) was the first to query respondents for this information, although only summary data survive. Beginning in 1970, however, the National Health Interview Surveys (NHIS) included this question in some polls. Answers from all the surveys were combined to produce a sample of more than 165,000 individuals. Using a respondent's age at the time of the survey and the reported age of initiation, [age they started smoking], the year the person began smoking could be determined. Dividing the number of adolescents (defined as those 12 to 17 years old) who started smoking during a particular interval by the number who were "eligible" to begin at the start of the interval set the initiation rate for that group.

D   Mass-marketing campaigns began as early as the 1880s, which boosted tobacco consumption sixfold by 1900. Much of the rise was attributed to a greater number of people smoking cigarettes, as opposed to using cigars, pipes, snuff or chewing tobacco. Marketing strategies included painted billboards and an extensive distribution of coupons, which a recipient could redeem for free cigarettes … . Some brands included soft-porn pictures of women in the packages. Such tactics inspired outcry from educational leaders concerned about their corrupting influence on teenage boys. Thirteen percent of the males surveyed in 1955 who reached adolescence between 1890 and 1910 commenced smoking by 18 years of age, compared with almost no females.

E   The power of targeted advertising is more apparent if one considers the men born between 1890 and 1899. In 1912, when many of these men were teenagers, the R.J. Reynolds company launched the Camel brand of cigarettes with a revolutionary approach. … Every city in the country was bombarded with print advertising. According to the 1955 CPS, initiation by age 18 for males in this group jumped to 21.6 percent, a two thirds increase over those born before 1890. The NHIS initiation rate also reflected this change. For adolescent males it went up from 2.9 percent between 1910 and 1912 to 4.9 percent between 1918 and 1921.

F   It was not until the mid-1920s that social mores permitted cigarette advertising to focus on women. … In 1926 a poster depicted women imploring smokers of Chesterfield cigarettes to "Blow Some My Way". The most successful crusade, however, was for Lucky Strikes, which urged women to "Reach for a Lucky instead of a Sweet." The 1955 CPS data showed that 7 percent of the women who were adolescents during the mid-1920s had started smoking by age 18, compared with only 2 percent in the preceding generation of female adolescents. Initiation rates from the NHIS data for adolescent girls were observed to increase threefold, from 0.6 percent between 1922 and 1925 to 1.8 percent between 1930 and 1933. In contrast, rates for males rose only slightly.

G   The next major boost in smoking initiation in adolescent females occurred in the late 1960s. In 1967 the tobacco industry launched "niche" brands aimed exclusively at women. The most popular was Virginia Slims. The visuals of this campaign emphasized a woman who was strong, independent and very thin. … Initiation in female adolescents nearly doubled, from 3.7 percent between 1964 and 1967 to 6.2 percent between 1972 and 1975 (NHIS data). During the same period, rates for adolescent males remained stable.

H   Thus, in four distinct instances over the past 100 years, innovative and directed tobacco marketing campaigns were associated with marked surges in primary demand from adolescents only in the target group. The first two were directed at males and the second two at females. Of course, other factors helped to entrench smoking in society. … Yet it is clear from the data that advertising has been an overwhelming force in attracting new users.

Questions 20–24

Do the following statements agree with the information in Reading Passage 2?
In boxes 20–24 write:

> **YES**   *if the statement is true according to the passage*
> **NO**   *if the statement contradicts the passage*
> **NOT GIVEN** *if there is no information about this in the passage*

20 Cigarette marketing has declined in the US since tobacco advertising was banned on TV.

21 Tobacco companies claim that their advertising targets existing smokers.

22 The difference in initiation rates between male and female smokers at the turn of the 19th century was due to selective marketing.

23 Women who took up smoking in the past lost weight.

24 The two surveys show different trends in cigarette initiation.

Questions 25–27

*Complete the sentences below with words taken from the Reading Passage. Use **NO MORE THAN THREE WORDS** for each answer. Write your answers in boxes 25–27 on your answer sheet.*

Tobacco companies are currently being accused of aiming their advertisements mainly at ... **(25)** ...

Statistics on smoking habits for men born between 1890 and 1899 were gathered in the year ... **(26)** ...

The ... **(27)** ... brand of cigarettes was designed for a particular sex.

READING PASSAGE 3

*You should spend about 20 minutes on **Questions 28–40** which are based on Reading Passage 3 below.*

The Pursuit of Happiness

New research uncovers some anti-intuitive insights into how many people are happy – and why.

Compared with misery, happiness is relatively unexplored terrain for social scientists. Between 1967 and 1994, 46,380 articles indexed in *Psychological Abstracts* mentioned depression, 36,851 anxiety, and 5,099 anger. Only 2,389 spoke of happiness, 2,340 life satisfaction, and 405 joy.

Recently we and other researchers have begun a systematic study of happiness. During the past two decades, dozens of investigators throughout the world have asked several hundred thousand representatively sampled people to reflect on their happiness and satisfaction with life – or what psychologists call "subjective well-being". In the US the National Opinion Research Center at the University of Chicago has surveyed a representative sample of roughly 1,500 people a year since 1957; the Institute for Social Research at the University of Michigan has carried out similar studies on a less regular basis, as has the Gallup Organization. Government-funded efforts have also probed the moods of European countries.

We have uncovered some surprising findings. People are happier than one might expect, and happiness does not appear to depend significantly on external circumstances. Although viewing life as a tragedy has a long and honorable history, the responses of random samples of people around the world about their happiness paints a much rosier picture. In the University of Chicago surveys, three in 10 Americans say they are very happy, for example. Only one in 10 chooses the most negative description "not too happy". The majority describe themselves as "pretty happy". …

How can social scientists measure something as hard to pin down as happiness? Most researchers simply ask people to report their feelings of happiness or unhappiness and to assess how satisfying their lives are. Such self-reported well-being is moderately consistent over years of retesting. Furthermore, those who say they are happy and satisfied seem happy to their close friends and family members and to a psychologist-interviewer. Their daily mood ratings reveal more positive emotions, and they smile more than those who call themselves unhappy. Self-reported happiness also predicts other indicators of well-being. Compared with the depressed, happy people are less self-focused, less hostile and abusive, and less susceptible to disease.

We have found that the even distribution of happiness cuts across almost all demographic classifications of age, economic class, race and educational level. In addition, almost all strategies for assessing subjective well-being – including those that sample people's experience by polling them at random times with beepers – turn up similar findings.

Interviews with representative samples of people of all ages, for example, reveal that no time of life is notably happier or unhappier. Similarly, men and women are equally likely to declare themselves "very

From "The Pursuit of Happiness" by David G. Myers and Ed Diener.

happy" and "satisfied" with life, according to a statistical digest of 146 studies by Marilyn J. Haring, William Stock and Morris A. Okun, all then at Arizona State University.

… Wealth is also a poor predictor of happiness. People have not become happier over time as their cultures have become more affluent. Even though Americans earn twice as much in today's dollars as they did in 1957, the proportion of those telling surveyors from the National Opinion Research Center that they are "very happy" has declined from 35 to 29 percent.

Even very rich people – those surveyed among *Forbes* magazine's 100 wealthiest Americans – are only slightly happier than the average American. Those whose income has increased over a 10-year period are not happier than those whose income is stagnant. Indeed, in most nations the correlation between income and happiness is negligible – only in the poorest countries, such as Bangladesh and India, is income a good measure of emotional well-being.

Are people in rich countries happier, by and large, than people in not so rich countries? It appears in general that they are, but the margin may be slim. In Portugal, for example, only one in 10 people reports being very happy, whereas in the much more prosperous Netherlands the proportion of very happy is four in 10. Yet there are curious reversals in this correlation between national wealth and well-being – the Irish during the 1980s consistently reported greater life satisfaction than the wealthier West Germans. Furthermore, other factors, such as civil rights, literacy and duration of democratic government, all of which also promote reported life satisfaction, tend to go hand in hand with national wealth. As a result, it is impossible to tell whether the happiness of people in wealthier nations is based on money or is a by-product of other felicities.

Although happiness is not easy to predict from material circumstances, it seems consistent for those who have it. In one National Institute on Aging study of 5,000 adults, the happiest people in 1973 were still relatively happy a decade later, despite changes in work, residence and family status.

Questions 28–30

*Choose the appropriate letters **A–D** and write them in boxes 28–30 on your answer sheet.*

28 What point are the writers making in the opening paragraph?
   A Happiness levels have risen since 1967.
   B Journals take a biased view on happiness.
   C Happiness is not a well-documented research area.
   D People tend to think about themselves negatively.

29 What do the writers say about their research findings?
   A They had predicted the results correctly.
   B They felt people had responded dishonestly.
   C They conflict with those of other researchers.
   D Happiness levels are higher than they had believed.

30 In the fourth paragraph, what does the reader learn about the research method used?
   A It is new.
   B It appears to be reliable.
   C It is better than using beepers.
   D It reveals additional information.

Questions 31–34

According to the passage, which of the findings below (31–34) is quoted by which Investigative Body (A–G)? Write your answers in boxes 31–34 on your answer sheet.

NB *There are more Investigative Bodies than findings, so you do not have to use all of them.*

31 Happiness is not gender related.

32 Over fifty per cent of people consider themselves to be 'happy'.

33 Happiness levels are marginally higher for those in the top income brackets.

34 'Happy' people remain happy throughout their lives.

Investigative Bodies

A The National Opinion Research Center, University of Chicago

B Arizona State University

C The Institute for Social Research, University of Michigan

D *Forbes* Magazine

E The National Institute on Aging

F The Gallup Organization

G The Government

Questions 35–40

Complete the summary of Reading Passage 3 below. Choose your answers from the box at the bottom of the page and write them in boxes 35–40 on your answer sheet.

NB *There are more words than spaces so you will not use them all. You may use any of the words more than once.*

HOW HAPPY ARE WE?

Example	*Answer*
Our happiness levels are ... **(0)** ... by relatively few factors.	affected

For example, incomes in the States have ... **(35)** ... over the past forty years but happiness levels have ... **(36)** ... over the same period. In fact, people on average incomes are only slightly ... **(37)** ... happy than extremely rich people and a gradual increase in prosperity makes ... **(38)** ... difference to how happy we are. In terms of national wealth, populations of wealthy nations are ... **(39)** ... happier than those who live in poorer countries. Although in some cases this trend is ... **(40)** ... and it appears that other factors need to be considered.

LIST OF WORDS

stopped	slightly	too	great
doubled	significant	similar	some
stabilised	remarkably	reversed	dropped
no	less	much	affected
crept up	slowed down	more	clearly

WRITING (Academic Module)

WRITING TASK 1

You should spend about 20 minutes on this task.

> *The charts below show the growth in the population of some of the world's largest cities.*
>
> *Write a report for a university lecturer describing the information shown below.*

You should write at least 150 words.

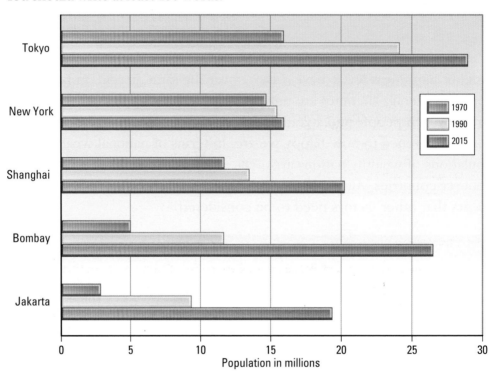

Population in millions

Top 5 biggest cities
By population (millions)

World Population
Billions

1950

1	New York	12.5
2	London	7.9
3	Tokyo	6.5
4	Paris	5.3
5	Moscow	5.3

2010

1	Tokyo	27.6
2	Bombay	26.6
3	Lagos	23.9
4	Shanghai	22.9
5	Jakarta	20.8

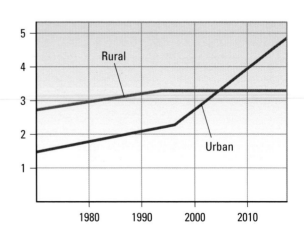

WRITING TASK 2

You should spend about 40 minutes on this task.

> *In most countries disabled people are not catered for adequately, e.g.*
> *buildings are often inappropriately designed. Governments rely too heavily*
> *on charities and voluntary organisations to provide assistance and funding.*
>
> *What further measures could be taken to assist disabled people?*
> *Discuss.*

You should use your own ideas, knowledge and experience and support your
arguments with examples and relevant evidence.

SECTION 1 *Questions 1–14*

*You are advised to spend 20 minutes on Questions **1–14**. First, read the text and answer Questions 1–9.*

Newtown Council

Dear Householder,

Recycling in your area

Are you doing all you can to recycle your rubbish? It only takes a minute to recycle and help reduce domestic waste as well as the costs of waste management. Here are some ideas to get you started.

Town Clerk

A   NEVER THROW AWAY VEGETABLE MATTER: START A COMPOST BIN IN YOUR GARDEN OR ON YOUR BALCONY. YOU'LL BE AMAZED HOW MUCH THIS CAN REDUCE THE BULK OF YOUR RUBBISH AND IT'S GREAT FOR THE GARDEN TOO.

B   DON'T THROW USED CONTAINERS IN THE RUBBISH. GET INTO THE HABIT OF SORTING THEM INTO RECYCLING CATEGORIES: GLASS, ALUMINIUM, PLASTIC AND PAPER.

C   GLASS CONTAINERS CAN BE PLACED IN THE BOTTLE BANKS AT SUPERMARKET CAR PARKS THROUGHOUT THE CITY. LOOK FOR THE BIG GREEN BINS. ALTERNATIVELY, LEAVE YOUR BOTTLES OUT FOR COLLECTION ON MONDAY MORNING.

D   ALUMINIUM CANS CAN EARN YOU CASH SO DON'T JUST THROW THEM AWAY – SAVE THEM AND SAVE MONEY. RING YOUR COUNCIL TO FIND OUT WHEN THEY COLLECT.

E   PAPER IS EASILY RECYCLED. WEEKLY COLLECTIONS ARE COMMON IN MOST AREAS. MAKE SURE YOU PLACE RECYCLABLE PAPER IN THE BLACK BINS PROVIDED. ASK AT THE COUNCIL OFFICES IF YOU DON'T ALREADY HAVE A BIN. BUT REMEMBER, WAXED PAPER IS NOT ACCEPTED.

F   MOST PLASTIC BOTTLES AND CONTAINERS CAN BE RECYCLED. LOOK ON THE BOTTOM OF THE CONTAINER FOR THE IDENTIFICATION CODE.

PET   HDPE   VINYL

MORE RECYCLING TIPS

The Council now includes vinyl bottles in their kerbside collection scheme. Here are some facts about vinyl.

• Vinyl (or PVC) is one of the three most commonly used plastics.

• About 80 per cent of the 180,000 tonnes of vinyl currently used in this country each year goes into long-life applications such as pipe and cable. About ten per cent is used in short-life products such as bottles and film wrap.

• Clear vinyl bottles are used for liquids such as fruit juice, mineral water and cooking oil. Coloured vinyl is used for products such as detergents and cosmetics.

• The identification code for vinyl is 13

Questions 1–4

Match the pictures below to the appropriate paragraph in the letter. Write the letters
A–F in the boxes 1–4 on your answer sheet.

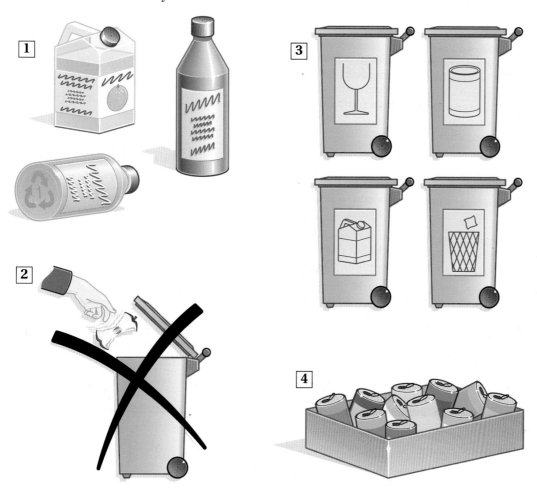

Questions 5–9

Look at the statements below. In boxes 5–9 on your answer sheet write

> **TRUE** *if the statement is true*
> **FALSE** *if the statement is false*
> **NOT GIVEN** *if the information is not given in the passage*

5 All paper can be recycled.

6 The council will collect paper on Mondays.

7 The recycling code is found on the side of plastic bottles.

8 Vinyl is mostly used for making bottles.

9 Non-drinkable liquids come in coloured vinyl bottles.

Join the Australian Museum Society and start enjoying the benefits

A As a Society member you can visit the Museum – considered to be one of the finest natural history museums in the world – absolutely free. A brilliant resource for adults and children, this museum offers you the opportunity to extend your understanding of our environment and cultural heritage through our superb collection of books and documents as well as the permanent and changing displays.

B The Society presents a diverse and interesting programme of Lectures – Seminars – Films – Social Events. You'll be invited to previews of all Museum exhibitions and have the chance to see exhibitions not usually open to the general public.

C Included in your membership is the award-winning magazine 'Nature Australia' which retails for $33 but comes to you as an exclusive membership privilege at no additional cost.

D Be part of the growth and development of the museum supporting its work in preserving our environment and heritage for generations to come. The Museum takes pride in the educational role it can play in helping young Australians to care for the environment.

E Embark on adventures! The Museum organises exciting and informative field trips to remote places led by scientists and specialists renowned in their fields. Previous trips have included destinations such as the Antarctic and Easter Island.

Questions 10–14

Look at the text about the Museum. There are five paragraphs A–E. From the list of headings below choose the most suitable heading for each paragraph. Write the appropriate numbers (i–vii) in boxes 10–14 on your answer sheet.

NB *There are more headings than paragraphs so you will not use them all. You may use any of the headings more than once.*

List of Headings

i	Family events
ii	Free gift
iii	Looking after the future
iv	Travel opportunities
v	World class collection of fossils
vi	Private viewings
vii	International reputation

10 Paragraph A

11 Paragraph B

12 Paragraph C

13 Paragraph D

14 Paragraph E

SECTION 2   *Questions 15–26*

You are advised to spend 20 minutes on Questions 15–26.

Questions 15–20

Read the information below and answer Questions 15–20.

TYPING COURSE

The university offers an annual keyboard skills course for all new students during orientation week. The course is designed to teach touch typing to people at the beginner's level, though experienced typists wishing to improve their skills may also benefit from the program. The course is computer based and draws on the latest findings in applied psychology to help you learn at your own pace. The method encourages the use of all ten fingers for maximum speed and accuracy and focuses on the need to establish good typing habits from the start.

The typing course is three courses in one. It teaches the alphabetic/numeric keyboard in eight structured lessons. Then the speed and accuracy lessons build your speed to whatever goals you choose. Finally the program teaches the numeric keypad in three simple lessons, particularly useful for spreadsheet work and entering statistical data. Participants each work at their own computer and are free to undertake the course in whatever order they choose. A qualified teacher who is thoroughly familiar with the program will be available at all times to explain the method and assist with any personal learning difficulties.

Two courses are available – come in and see us now!

IMPROVE YOUR SKILLS AT THE COMPUTER CENTRE

HOW TO ENROL

Typing courses are held at the Computer Centre in the Wilson Building. Tuition is free but there is a nominal charge for the accompanying book which you will need to purchase. Intensive courses begin every morning during orientation week at 9.00 am Monday to Friday. To qualify for a place, you must show your student card when you enrol. Places are limited, so get in early!

ADVANCED WORD PROCESSING SKILLS COURSE

Monday evenings from 5.00–7.00 pm

Gain an understanding of the concepts and skills of word processing. Learn how to create and edit a document, recall documents from disk and other important skills. Familiarity with a PC computer keyboard and a mouse is essential, plus an ability to touch type. To enrol please complete a form and leave it at the Reception Desk. Classes are free but there is a nominal charge for the use of paper and disks.

Questions 15–16

*Choose the appropriate letters **A–D** and write them in boxes 15–16 on your answer sheet.*

15 The typing course is aimed at
    A people with no experience.
    B a mixed level group.
    C experienced typists.
    D computing students.

16 The typing course
    A takes three full days.
    B consists of three lessons.
    C is divided into three parts.
    D requires at least three hours.

Questions 17–20

In boxes 17–20 on your answer sheet write

    TRUE   *if the statement is true*
    FALSE   *if the statement is false*
    NOT GIVEN *if no information is given about this*

Example	Answer
Using a computer to learn has made typing much easier.	NOT GIVEN

17 The typing course is available every year.

18 Touch typing is an essential skill for university.

19 The Advanced Word Processing course takes place once a week.

20 There are no costs involved in doing either of the courses.

Questions 21–26

*Look at the information about activities on the University Open Day. Which place would you visit for the following reasons? Write the appropriate letter **A–H** in boxes 21–26 on your answer sheet. You may use any letter more than once.*

Example	Answer
You are interested in finding out about sporting facilities.	G

21 You may be interested in living in on campus.

22 You want to buy something to remind you of your visit today.

23 You want to listen to some music during the day.

24 You are interested in the history of the settlement of Australia.

25 You want to attend a course to improve your reading speed.

26 You want to have a hot meal at lunch time.

UNIVERSITY COLLEGE

UNIVERSITY COLLEGE OPEN DAY

In addition to the mini lectures and talks taking place across campus on Saturday, there are a number of other ways to find out about university life.

A Fielder Library will be open from 9.00 to 5.00. This library is one of the largest libraries in Australia and is proud of its outstanding collection of specialist books and learning resources. The Library's Rare Books Collection features an exhibition on Australian Explorers of the 18th and 19th Centuries.

B Guided tours of the Language Centre and Computer Laboratories will be running during the day. You are welcome to try out the excellent technical facilities of the Language Centre. Tours leave at 11.00, 1.00 and 3.00 from the reception area at the main entrance. Find out about Study Skills programs and free English classes.

C The university has three museums. The Nuttall Museum situated near the Quad, with its collection of classical archaeological exhibits and ancient pottery, the University Art Gallery and the McCaulay Museum of Natural History are open all day.

D Residential college life is fun and rewarding and the best way to make friends in your first year at university. Tours of the colleges run throughout the day. Ask at the Colleges Information Booth for tour times and the cost of living in.

E The University Union's Contact Information Desk and campus store in the Hart Building will be open from 9.00. T-shirts, diaries, bags and university souvenirs will be on sale. Sandwiches and drinks are also available.

F Interactive displays and exhibits by Chemistry, Mathematics, Biology, Physics and Psychology departments will be held throughout the day in the Chemistry building. Come in and talk to us about our courses and your areas of interest.

G The new University College Sports and Aquatic Centre includes an Olympic pool, tennis courts, fitness centre, sports hall, squash courts and sports bar. Tours of the Sports Centre depart from the Information Booth in the centre of the Quad at 10.15, 12.15 and 2.15.

H A variety of hot and cold food will be available throughout the day in the Hart Building. The University Jazz Society will perform in the bar from 10.30 and a debate will be held in the main hall from 1.00 to 2.00.

SECTION 3   *Questions 27–40*

You are advised to spend about 20 minutes on Questions 27–40.
Read the following text and answer Questions 27–40.

300-year-old secrets of Stradivarius

Stradivarius violins can cost £2 million. Does their sound match their price? Julian Brown asks what a 17ᵗʰ century craftsman knew that modern instrument makers are only just discovering.

Antonio Stradivari was born in 1644, into a respected family of craftsmen in Cremona, a northern Italian town that was already famed far afield for its violins.

Stradivari was apprenticed to the instrument maker Nicolò Amati at around the age of 12 and by the time he died, aged 93, he had made around a thousand violins and at least 300 other stringed instruments, including cellos, lutes and guitars.

A productive life, certainly, and a reasonably well-rewarded one: he sold most of his output for the equivalent of around £4 each, and appeared well satisfied with the moderate, middle-class income and lifestyle his craft brought him and his family. Stradivari could never have dreamt that, 250 years after his death, his violins are auctioned and reach prices anywhere from £200,000 to several million.

What makes a Stradivarius violin so valuable? That's a question that continues to intrigue musicians, scientists and the public to this day. For decades, scientists and violin makers have tried to establish the Stradivarius's "secrets".

During his career, Stradivari made certain subtle changes in the proportions of the violin, gradually increasing the instrument's power. While his early work followed the traditions of his teacher Amati, by the close of the 17ᵗʰ century the Stradivarius had become flatter and broader and the bridge began to look much as it does today.

But violin makers have long copied the proportions of Stradivarius's instruments without achieving the same results. So the secret must lie elsewhere. But where? In the deep, lustrous auburn-red varnish, according to one theory. But there's a problem. Strads have withstood nearly 300 years of wear and tear. Not surprisingly, the rich varnish on many of them has taken a battering and, in some cases, most of it has been worn away. Yet these instruments still sound magnificent.

In the 1980s a US researcher came up with a new theory: the secret lay in the wood. Stradivari used wood – maple and spruce – that was delivered to Cremona by being floated along the Italian canals; perhaps the contact with water had changed its character. The idea was initially supported by electron microscope pictures of the violin's surface: Strad wood was found to be riddled with tiny, open pores, while those of modern instruments were tightly closed.

But later research suggested that whether the pores showed as open or closed under examination was not dependent on the violin at all, but rather on how the wood sample had been cut and prepared before it was examined under microscopy.

Electron microscopy, however, may yet provide the answer. Recent research in Cambridge has found a layer beneath the Strad's famed varnish. Under the electron microscope it appears like a seam of marzipan sandwiched between the cake of wood and the icing-like varnish. Claire Barlow and Jim Woodhouse, who work in Cambridge University's Engineering Department, were able to obtain a few small samples of wood taken from Strads and other old instruments that were undergoing restoration. They subjected the middle layer to spectroscopic x-ray analysis to find out what it contained. The results varied from sample to sample, but they all contained a range of minerals including aluminium, silicon, phosphorous and calcium.

This turns out to be consistent with another idea put forward in the 1980s. For some time experts had been arguing over whether the craftsmen of Cremona had used some kind of wood sealant before applying varnish to the instruments they were making.

John Chipura, an American geologist and violin enthusiast, published a letter in the magazine *The Strad* suggesting that this sealant may well have been a layer of Roman cement. Readily available, the cement was made from local materials including volcanic ash, whose mineral constituents are very similar to those revealed by Barlow and Woodhouse's spectroscopic analysis.

Even so, Barlow is reluctant to draw any firm conclusions about the purpose of the layer. "It's tempting to think that it might have been applied as a sealant, or to provide a smooth surface on which you could varnish easily. But these layers are much thicker than you'd need to do either of those things. They were put on for some purpose that we still don't really understand."

Barlow's collaborator, Jim Woodhouse, has spent many years studying the acoustics of violins and he was interested to find out what effect the mineral layer would have on the sound quality of the instruments.

"Virtually any treatment of the wood, such as a preservative or varnish, will change the vibrational properties of the violin and therefore its sound," he explains. "We have taken flat plates of spruce and varnished them with various combinations of finishes, but the differences in the vibrational properties we found were really rather subtle. So there may be an effect, but it's not immediately obvious."

Undoubtedly Stradivari was a supreme craftsman, but the secret of his genius may not lie in one aspect of his craftsmanship but in a combination of factors. "To make a violin you've got to do a great many things right and in harmony with one another," says Woodhouse. "If there is a secret to the Stradivarius sound, it is in achieving a perfect balance."

Questions 27–33

Complete the summary of the reading passage below. Choose your answers from the box at the bottom of the page and write them in boxes 27–33 on your answer sheet.

NB *There are more words than spaces so you will not use them all.*
You may use any of the words more than once.

The Stradivarius Violin

Example	*Answer*
Stradivari made his first violins in the traditional ... **(0)** ...	*style*

of his teacher, Nicolo Amati. Later models had different ... **(27)** ..., becoming flatter and broader, and people believed this accounted for their special sound. But subsequent ... **(28)** ... of the Stradivarius failed to demonstrate this. Another theory was that the ... **(29)** ... had a special effect on the instrument. However, many Stradivarius violins have lost this and yet still retain their special musical qualities. An American researcher claimed that the method of ... **(30)** ... had resulted in a change in the ... **(31)** ... of the wood and this theory was supported at first, then later rejected. The most up-to-date research is investigating a ... **(32)** ... of material that has been found within the violin which may affect the ... **(33)** ... of the Stradivarius.

LIST OF WORDS

colour	composition	transportation	construction
varnish	sound	proportions	violins
style	wood	layer	copies
sample	music	instruments	vibrations

Questions 34–36

*The diagram below shows a cross section of a Stradivarius violin. Complete the labels on the diagram by selecting **NO MORE THAN THREE WORDS** from the Reading Passage to fill each numbered space. Write your answers in boxes 34–36 on your answer sheet.*

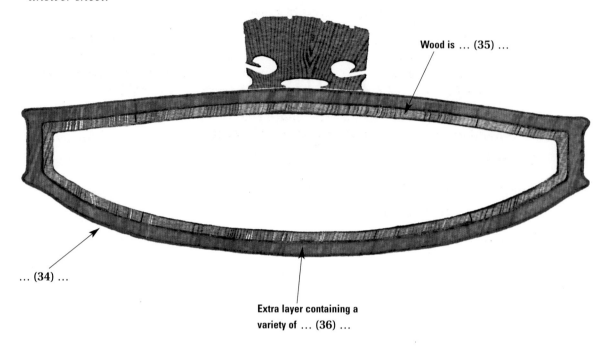

Wood is ... (35) ...

... (34) ...

Extra layer containing a variety of ... (36) ...

Questions 37–40

*Using **NO MORE THAN THREE WORDS** answer the following questions. Write your answers in boxes 37–40 on your answer sheet.*

37 How much did Stradivari receive for each violin he made?

38 What natural material did John Chipura suggest was used in making the Stradivarius violin?

39 What quality of the layers makes Claire Barlow doubt their function as a sealant?

40 According to Jim Woodhouse, what might be the key to Stradivari's genius?

WRITING (General Training Module)

WRITING TASK 1

You should spend about 20 minutes on this task.

> *You live in a flat and you have a tenancy agreement which states that you must give three months' notice when you wish to leave. You have paid a deposit of two months' rent. Now a member of your family has a problem and you need to give up your flat and return home as soon as possible.*
>
> *Write a letter to your landlady. Explain your circumstances, tell her what you intend to do and ask her for special consideration.*

You should write at least 150 words.

You do not need to write your own address.

Begin your letter as follows:

Dear ....,

WRITING TASK 2

You should spend about 40 minutes on this task.

As part of a class assignment you have to write about the following topic:

> **Coins and paper money will soon be replaced by credit and bank cards.**
>
> **Eventually we will have a cashless society which will be safer and more convenient for everyone.**
>
> **Do you agree or disagree?**

You should write at least 250 words.

You should use your own ideas, knowledge and experience and support your arguments with examples and relevant evidence.

SPEAKING

Describe a children's story that you know well.

You should say:

- ♦ when you first heard or read it
- ♦ what you particularly liked about it
- ♦ why you think it became popular

Possible follow-up questions are:

Do you think this story is as popular now as it used to be?
Do you think many other adults like this story too?

Describe a family celebration that you once attended.

You should say:

- ♦ where it took place
- ♦ why it was held
- ♦ how you felt about it

Possible follow-up questions are:

Are celebrations of this type common?
Do you think that celebrations of this type are important?

Recording Script

Words *in italics* indicate the location of answers to the listening exercises.

UNIT 1, EXTRACT 1

Example

ASSISTANT	Can I help you?
WOMAN	Yes, *I'm looking for a tie for my husband.* Where would I find the men's department?
ASSISTANT	On the first floor. You can take the lift or the escalator.
WOMAN	Thank you very much.
ASSISTANT	You're welcome.

1

WAITER	Can I take your coat?
WOMAN	Thank you.
WAITER	And *would you like something to drink before you order your meal*?
WOMAN	Yes, please. Can we see the wine list?
WAITER	Certainly.

2

POLICE OFFICER	Can I see your licence please, sir?
DRIVER	Yes, uh … certainly.
POLICE OFFICER	Did you know you were *exceeding the speed limit* when you came over the hill just now? *Our radar registered* that you were travelling at 157 km an hour.
DRIVER	Oh, really? I hadn't realised.
POLICE OFFICER	There's an on the spot *fine of $280.00* for that, I'm afraid, sir.

3

HUSBAND	I'm afraid I got stopped by the police for speeding today, dear.
WIFE	Oh no, *David*. You didn't, did you!
HUSBAND	Yes, *I got a fine of $280.00* – on the spot.
WIFE	That's dreadful. We can't afford that. You really should drive more slowly!

4

LECTURER	Now I'd just like to recap on what we were talking about last week *before going ahead with this week's lecture.* We were, if I remember rightly, looking at the main causes of the Second World War and *I'd just like to go back to some of the points I made.* But first, does anyone have any questions?

5

STUDENT	How do I go about *joining the Table Tennis Club*?
ADMIN	You need to *fill in this form and show me your student card.*
STUDENT	Is there a fee?
ADMIN	Yes, there's a joining fee of $15.00 and an annual subscription of $10.

6

STUDENT	I'm afraid *I haven't been able to finish the history essay,* and I was hoping that *you would give me an extension.*
LECTURER	When do you think you could let me have it?
STUDENT	Well … I should be able to finish it by next Monday.
LECTURER	Well …, OK. As long as I can have it by then. That'll be fine.

7

STUDENT A	Did you manage to *finish the history essay*?
STUDENT B	*No. Did you*?
STUDENT A	No. I couldn't find the books in the library.
STUDENT B	No, neither could I. But fortunately the lecturer has given me an extension. You should go and see her. She's very helpful.

8

FLIGHT ATTENDANT: *Would you like something to drink with your meal? Drinks are complementary on this flight.*

PASSENGER: I'll just have a soft drink thanks. Can I have a Coke?

FLIGHT ATTENDANT: Oh, I'm sorry. I'll have to go and get you one when I've finished serving this row.

PASSENGER: Oh, OK.

9

DOCTOR: Morning, *Mr White*. Come in. And what can I do for you today?

PATIENT: Well *doctor, I'm having difficulty sleeping.* I often wake up at 3.00 in the morning and I just can't get back to sleep.

DOCTOR: I see … and how long has this been going on?

PATIENT: Oh, about a month now. I wonder if you could prescribe something.

10

PRINCIPAL: *Good morning, everybody.* Now, first of all I'd like to start by *welcoming you all to the college.* We're delighted to have you here and we hope you are going to enjoy your stay with us. My name is Mary Smithers and *I'm the college principal.*

UNIT 2, EXTRACT 1

A Oh hi, everybody. It's Julia here. It's Thursday afternoon. I'm just ringing to confirm dinner *on Friday night.* I'll be there *about 7.30.* Can't wait to see you all!

B Johnson's Repairs here. Your *video recorder* is now ready for collection. There is a *charge of £50.00* to be paid when you come and pick it up.

C Message for Mary Brooks. This is the *University Bookshop* here. The book you ordered on Asian Economies is not available. I'm afraid it's *out of print.* Sorry about that. Let me know what you want us to do.

D Hi. This is Nick. I've left my *football boots* at home today and I desperately need them for the match this afternoon. If someone gets this message, could you please bring them into the college *before 12 o'clock.* The new boots, not the old boots. Thanks a lot, see you …

E Dr Boyd's surgery here. I'm afraid we'll have to cancel Ms Taylor's appointment tomorrow, as unfortunately *Dr Boyd has the flu.* Could she come on *Monday at 3.30 pm* instead and ring back to confirm she can make that time?

F Oh, hello – message for Mr Lee. Newport supermarkets here. I believe you lost *a pair of glasses* yesterday. We've found a pair at the checkout. We're keeping them at *the customer service desk.* Would you like to come in and see if they're yours?

G Hello – this is Sam. Message for Nick. We're having *a farewell party for Prof. Hall* on Saturday. You know he's going to China for two years. Give us a ring on *9818 4078.*

UNIT 2, EXTRACT 2

CLERK: Good Morning, Blue Harbour Cruises. How can I help you?

TOURIST: Oh, uh, good morning. Um … can you tell me something about the different cruises you run?

CLERK: Well … we run three cruises every day, each offering something slightly different.

TOURIST: Let me just get a pencil so I can make a note of this. Right.

CLERK: Firstly, there's the Highlight Cruise, … then we do the Noon Cruise and we also have our *Coffee Cruise.*

TOURIST: Um … could you tell me a bit about them? When they leave, how often, that sort of thing?

CLERK: Well, the Highlight Cruise is $16 per person, and that *leaves at 9.30 every morning* and takes two hours to go round the harbour.

TOURIST	Right … 9.30. And do you get coffee or refreshments?
CLERK	No, but there's a kiosk on board where you can buy drinks and snacks. And we do provide everyone with *a free souvenir postcard*.
TOURIST	Right.
CLERK	And then there's our Noon Cruise at *$42 per person*. This is more expensive but, of course, it takes longer and for that price you get *a three-course lunch*.
TOURIST	Oh, that sounds good … And what about the last one?
CLERK	That's the Coffee Cruise. Well, that's $25 each. It takes two and a half hours.
TOURIST	When does that leave?
CLERK	*At a quarter past two daily.*
TOURIST	And presumably the coffee is included?
CLERK	Yes, and *sandwiches are served free of charge*.

TOURIST	I think the Coffee Cruise would suit us best, as lunch is included at the hotel. Can I book for two people for tomorrow, please?
CLERK	No need to book. Just be down at the quay at 2 o'clock. All our cruises depart from Jetty No. 2.
TOURIST	Can you tell me where that is exactly?
CLERK	Yes, No. 2 Jetty is *opposite the shops*. It's clearly signposted.
TOURIST	Right … and can you tell me, is there a commentary?
CLERK	Yes, there's a commentary on all the cruises.
TOURIST	Is it possible to listen to the commentary in Japanese? My friend doesn't speak much English.
CLERK	It's *in English only*, I'm afraid, but the tour guides usually speak some Japanese, so she'll be able to ask questions.
TOURIST	Oh fine.
CLERK	Oh and one other thing – I should just mention that it gets extremely hot on the upper deck at this time of year, so it's a good idea to *wear a hat*. Otherwise you could get quite badly sunburned.
TOURIST	Right. I'll remember that. Thanks very much.

UNIT 2, EXTRACT 3

CLERK	Good morning, Golden Wheels Car Rentals. How can I help you?
MAN	Yes, good morning. I'd like to hire a car, please.
CLERK	Can I just get your name, sir?
MAN	Yes, *Frank Moorcroft*.
CLERK	Could you spell that please?
MAN	Yes, Frank – F R A N K, Moorcroft – M double O R C R O F T
CLERK	And the address?
MAN	My home address?
CLERK	Yes, sir. We need your home address.
MAN	Oh right. OK, Flat 26, *19 Lake Road*, Richmond.
CLERK	And your telephone number there?
MAN	*3697 4500.*
CLERK	Are you the holder of a current driver's licence?
MAN	Yes, I am.
CLERK	Could I have the number please, sir?
MAN	Just let me find it. Here we are. *UT 9128.*
CLERK	Right, now what kind of vehicle were you looking for?
MAN	I was thinking of doing some off-road driving.
CLERK	When did you want to collect the vehicle?
MAN	Tomorrow, if that's possible.
CLERK	*Tomorrow's the 23rd June.* Well, all the four-wheel drives are out, but we've got a nice *family-sized vehicle* – a Ford. I could let you have that in the morning. Almost as good as a four-wheel drive.
MAN	OK. I'll take that. What is the cost of the Ford?
CLERK	Well, the daily rate is $70, but it's only $50 a day if you have it for more than three days.
MAN	*I'll need it for the whole week.*
CLERK	OK and there's an additional $15 for insurance which brings it up to *$65.00*. We do recommend that you take the insurance.
MAN	Right, so that's a total of $65 a day, not $50.

CLERK	Yes, sir, that's correct, and would you like to collect it from our city branch or at the airport or your hotel?
MAN	I can pick it up *in the city*.
CLERK	And how will you be paying for that? Cash, cheque or credit card?
MAN	Do you take traveller's cheques?
CLERK	No, sorry.
MAN	I'll pay *by credit card* then.
CLERK	Right, thank you very much. We'll see you in the morning, sir.

UNIT 3, EXTRACT 1

JILL	Hello, Sue … fancy meeting you here! It is Sue Johnson, isn't it?
SUE	Oh, hi, Jill. It must be ages since we've seen each other. What a surprise! How *are* you?
JILL	Yes, well, … I'm fine … just got back from two years' teaching in Hong Kong, actually.
SUE	I thought you'd gone into computing or nursing.
JILL	No, *I ended up being a teacher after all …* And how about you?
SUE	Oh, fine. Things are going quite well in fact.
JILL	So what've you been up to over the last three years?
SUE	Working, studying, you know the usual things … Oh, and I got married last year.
JILL	Congratulations! Anyone I know?
SUE	Yeah, you might remember him from our college days. Do you remember Gerry? Gerry Fox?
JILL	Gerry … Was he the one with the dark hair and beard?
SUE	No, that was Sam. No, *Gerry's got blond hair and glasses*. He's pretty tall. Well, we got married … finally …
JILL	Great, and where did the wedding take place? Was it here in London?
SUE	No, in the end we decided to get married in Scotland. Gerry's parents live there, so we were married in the *small village church, with the mountains in the background*.
JILL	Fabulous. Have you got any pictures?

SUE	Well, funny you should ask … I have actually got a couple here. They're a bit battered because I've been carrying them around in my bag.
JILL	Oh, never mind. Let's have a look. Oh, don't you look wonderful! Who are those people behind you?
SUE	That's my older sister Clara.
JILL	Oh, she looks like you.
SUE	Do you think so? Everyone says that, but *we* can't see it.
JILL	Is she married now?
SUE	Yes, and she's got three children: *a girl and twin boys* as well.
JILL	Wow – imagine having twins!
SUE	Look, why don't we have dinner together and catch up on a few things? Would you like to come over one evening?
JILL	That'd be lovely.
SUE	What about next Friday evening?
JILL	Fine. What time? Shall I come over about 8 o'clock?
SUE	Oh, *come about half past seven*. I'm usually home around 6.30 so that'd give me plenty of time to get dinner ready.
JILL	Fine, and one last thing … where do you live? What's the address?
SUE	Oh, good thinking … here's my card, the address is on the back. We've got *a flat in an old house*. We live on *the third floor of a large old house*. The house has been converted into flats. You know, it's a typical London flat. So when you arrive you'll need to *press the bell second from the top*.
JILL	The bell second from the top. OK.
SUE	There's a little intercom arrangement so I can let you in.
JILL	Right. OK, see you on Friday then.

UNIT 4, EXTRACT 1

WOMAN A	Guess who I saw today?
WOMAN B	Who?
WOMAN A	I ran into our old English teacher, Mr Britton, in the supermarket.
WOMAN B	Really?

WOMAN A — Funny thing is – I didn't recognise him. He tapped me on the shoulder and I wondered who on earth it was! He's grown a beard and he looks quite different.

1

ASSISTANT — Can I help you?

STUDENT — Yes, well, I bought this tie last week for my boyfriend's birthday and um, well, he doesn't like it. Could I change it for something else?

ASSISTANT — Certainly, madam, provided that it hasn't been worn and that you have the receipt.

STUDENT — Yes, here it is.

ASSISTANT — OK … um … this tie looks as if it's been worn, I'm afraid. I can't put that back on the rack.

STUDENT — Oh … that's a pity.

2

WIFE — You know, John, I'm getting quite worried about Maria.

HUSBAND — Why – what's happened?

WIFE — Well, I was speaking to her teacher today after school. She tells me that Maria often doesn't finish her homework and when she does … well … the standard is often pretty poor.

HUSBAND — Maybe I'd better have a word with her then.

3

NEWSREADER — And now, closer to home and the health service … The prime minister announced today that the Government would be looking at ways of reducing hospital waiting lists in Australian hospitals. At present patients can wait up to two years for a hospital bed for operations not considered to be life-threatening. A spokesperson for St Michael's Hospital said some patients wait for over two years for operations such as hip replacements and other so-called minor surgery.

4

STUDENT A — Now, … about this picnic. Where are we going to go?

STUDENT B — Well, I thought we might all meet up at the Opera House at two o'clock and walk through the Botanical Gardens and find a nice spot down near the water. What do you think?

STUDENT B — Great!

5

STUDENT A — You know the computing assignment we've got?

STUDENT B — Yeah!

STUDENT A — Have you finished yours yet?

STUDENT B — No … have you?

STUDENT A — No, that's why I asked. I'm having a lot of difficulty understanding the topic.

STUDENT B — Why don't we go and see the lecturer about it and ask him? He's a pretty friendly sort of guy. I'm sure he won't mind.

STUDENT A — Good idea.

6

STUDENT — Excuse me … I'm trying to find a copy of *A Guide to English Grammar* – I can't find it on the shelf.

LIBRARIAN — Let me have a look. It may be waiting to be put back on the shelves. Hold on a minute. …Yes, it came back in this morning, but a couple of people have reserved it already. Would you like to reserve it after that?

STUDENT No, thanks – I think I'll go and buy a copy for myself!

7

ASSISTANT Hey! You guys! Could you two stop playing on the walking machine? It's not a toy, you know.

TEENAGER Oh sorry. We were just trying it out. Isn't that what it's for?

ASSISTANT If you're not going to buy it, you shouldn't use it!

TEENAGER Well, we don't know whether we're going to buy it if we don't try it, do we?

8

VICE CHANCELLOR Good afternoon, distinguished guests, family and friends and students of this university. I'd like to extend a very warm welcome to you all and say how pleasing it is to see such a good turnout of parents and friends at today's graduation ceremony which is, in my opinion, a most important day in the university calendar.

UNIT 4, EXTRACT 2

PRESENTER
Hello and welcome to this week's edition of *Tell me more* – the programme where you ask the questions and we provide the answers. And we've had a wide variety of questions from you this week.

And the subject we've picked for you this week in response to your many letters is the production of postage stamps. And as usual, we've been doing our homework on the subject.

So who designs the postage stamps that we stick on our letters? Well in Australia the design of postage stamps is in the hands of Australia Post. In Britain, it's the Royal Mail that looks after stamps and it seems that both countries have a similar approach to the production process.

We discovered to our surprise that *it can take up to two years to produce a new postage stamp.* Why's that I hear you ask! Surely it can't be all that difficult to design a stamp? In fact, it isn't. But it seems it's *a lengthy business.* Firstly they have to choose the subjects and this is done with the help of market research. Members of the general public, including families, are surveyed to find out what sort of things they would like to see on their stamps. *They are given a list of possible topics and asked to rank them.*

A list is then presented to the Advisory Committee which meets about once a month. The committee is made up of outside designers, graphic artists and stamp collectors. If the committee likes the list, it sends it up to *the Board of Directors which makes the final decision.* Then they commission an artist. In Australia artists *are paid $1,500 for a stamp design and a further $800 if the committee actually decides to use the design.* So there's a possibility that a stamp might be designed, but still never actually go into circulation.

So what kind of topics are acceptable? Well, the most important thing is that *they must be of national interest.* And because a stamp needs to represent the country in some way, characters from books are popular, or you often find national animals and birds. So of course, the kangaroo is a favourite in Australia. With the notable exception of members of the British royal family, *no living people ever appear* on Australian or British stamps. This policy is under review, but many stamp enthusiasts see good reason for keeping it that way to avoid the possibility of people in power using their influence to get onto the stamps.

Every year the Royal Mail in Britain receives about 2000 ideas for stamps but very few of them are ever used. *One favourite topic is kings and queens;* for instance King Henry VIII, famous for his six wives, has recently appeared on a British stamp together with a stamp featuring each of his wives.

But despite the extensive research which is done before a stamp is produced, it seems *it's hard to please everybody,* and apparently all sorts of people write to the post office to say that they loved or hated a particular series. The stamp to cause the most concern ever in Australia was a picture of Father Christmas surfing at the beach. And when you consider that the practical function of a stamp is only as a receipt for postage, *I think perhaps the importance accorded to stamps has got out of all proportion!*

Well, that's all for today. If there's a subject you want us to tell you more about, drop us a line at …

UNIT 5, EXTRACT 1

GIRL	Mum! What do you think of my new shirt? Do you like it?
WOMAN	Oh, it's … uh … lovely, darling.
Girl	Oh Mum.
NARRATOR	*Did* the woman like the shirt? The answer is No.

1

MAN	Fantastic! This is the first day I've had off for months and look at the weather. Would you believe it?
WOMAN	Oh well. At least you've got the day to yourself. Never mind the weather.
NARRATOR	Is the weather fine?

2

STUDENT A	Hi, Sue. It's Mario here.
STUDENT B	Oh, hi. How are you?
STUDENT A	Fine – look I was wondering if you were free on Saturday evening. I've got some tickets for a concert. Would you like to come?
STUDENT B	Oh, look, I'm sorry … I'd really like to, but … like … I'm studying for my exams at the moment, and well … I'm sorry … I can't.
STUDENT A	OK – not to worry. Some other time then, I suppose.
STUDENT B	Right … sure …
NARRATOR	Is the girl trying to avoid the date?

3

CUSTOMER	I bought this mobile phone on Friday …
ASSISTANT	Is there a problem with it, sir?
CUSTOMER	Well, primarily, it does not appear to function outside the metropolitan area, which means it fails to function as a mobile phone as far as I can see.
ASSISTANT	Right, I'll just have a word with the manager and see what we can do.
NARRATOR	Was the man satisfied with the phone?

4

REPORTER	Excuse me, Minister. Can you tell us whether your government intends to increase student university fees in the next budget?
POLITICIAN	The government has every intention of ensuring that students will not be disadvantaged by any increase in fees which it may be necessary to introduce, by offering grants and scholarships to students wherever possible.
NARRATOR	Are university fees going to rise?

5

MAN	I've just ordered a new MMX computer with 32-speed CD ROM; I'm getting it tomorrow.
WOMAN	That's great.
MAN	It's twice the speed of the one we've got now and much better for games.
WOMAN	Can't wait to see it.
NARRATOR	Does the woman want to see the computer?

6

MOTHER	What did the doctor have to say?
SON	Well, she said if I want to get rid of this flu I should stay in bed for the next three days, drink plenty of orange juice and stay nice and warm.
MOTHER	That means you'll miss your football on Saturday.
SON	No, I should be OK by Saturday.

MOTHER	Oh, OK? Too sick for school, but OK for football, eh?
SON	Mum, that's not fair.
NARRATOR	Is the boy very sick?

7

WOMAN	I've just seen the new Bond movie.
MAN	Have you? I saw it on Saturday .
WOMAN	Wasn't it fabulous? Didn't you just love the special effects?
MAN	Yeah, they weren't bad. It was OK.
NARRATOR	Did the woman like the movie?

8

TEACHER	Michael, did you do this work yourself?
STUDENT	Yes, sir. Of course I did.
TEACHER	It seems to have been remarkably well done, for you!
STUDENT	Guess I had a good day, sir.
TEACHER	Michael, I wasn't born yesterday.
STUDENT	No, sir.
NARRATOR	Is the teacher pleased with the boy's work?

UNIT 5, EXTRACT 2

RICHARD	Sue, who was that at the door?
SUE	Oh, someone *collecting money for the local hospital* again.
FRANK	Did you give them anything?
SUE	No, Frank, I did *not*. I refuse to give money at the door to people – it annoys me the way they come round here on Sunday morning, expecting us to donate money all the time.
RICHARD	Well, they're hardly likely to come round during the week, are they? 'Cos anybody who can afford to donate money will be out at work! Anyway, Sue, I think they just make you feel guilty.
SUE	Richard, I beg your pardon!
RICHARD	You don't want to give any money, so you turn the situation round and blame them for knocking on your door.
SUE	Richard, that's not true! I'm happy to give money but through the official channels. I just don't like people coming to my door.
FRANK	Well … I tend to agree with Sue. *I don't see why we should have to pay for the new hospital out of our pockets.* We already pay our taxes – income tax, purchase tax, you name it tax. *The government should pay for the hospital* out of general revenue – not the local residents.
SUE	Yes, that's right. I mean – perhaps we don't need a hospital in this area anyway. Why can't people go to the General Hospital in town? They've got all the facilities there.
FRANK	Ah, but Sue. The day you need a hospital, you'll want it there ready and waiting for you, close to home, not miles away. And besides, other people may not be able to travel into town like you. Old people, people without cars …
SUE	Oh Frank, you know what I mean. Anyway, I still think that the government should pay for this kind of thing.
RICHARD	*That's because you've grown up in a system where the state does everything for you from the cradle to the grave. But, it doesn't work like that any more; the party's over, I'm afraid,* because there simply isn't enough money left in the bank to pay for all this stuff. You see, we're an …
SUE	Yes, but *most of the time they waste it.* I mean, look at how much government money is spent on roads, on airports, on huge hotels, on space research, for instance, instead of on local social issues. If they …
FRANK	Well, I'm sorry but I can't agree with you there. Firstly, hotels are built privately, with private money, not government money, and as for space research … well, I think it's incredibly important.
SUE	Why, Frank? Tell me … *why* is space research so important?
FRANK	Because it's pushing back the frontiers of science … quite literally … and also because you get some fantastic discoveries made as a result of this kind of research *and they have an immediate effect on our day to day lives.*

RICHARD	Such as non-stick teflon frying pans.
FRANK	Well yes, but there are other much more relevant examples – high speed aircraft, for instance, navigational equipment, thermal clothing, all sorts of things.
RICHARD	Nice to think that your up to date skiing clothes were originally designed for astronauts.
SUE	Oh Richard, you are such a cynic.
FRANK	Well, you guys can laugh, but *I bet you by the year 2050, people will actually be shooting off to Mars on their holidays*, to get away from it all!
SUE	No thanks. Not me!
FRANK	You think I'm joking, don't you? The next great explorers of this world will be the astronauts. People with vision and courage to try and find new territories. You think it's just science fiction, but it isn't. It's real.
SUE	Well I still think the government would be better advised to target some of the problems on this earth before they go shooting off to Mars. How can we possibly talk about space travel when there is youth unemployment, crime, poverty…? That's where our energy should be going … into making sure that people have a roof over their heads and employment *because work gives people a sense of self.* No one wants to be on the receiving end of charity all the time.
RICHARD	Here we go again. *Lots of fine ideals, but …*
SUE	Richard, you have to have ideals. Otherwise what's the point?
FRANK	Yeah, I agree with Sue. I think she's right.
RICHARD	I don't know.

UNIT 6, EXTRACT 1

1

Incoming governments often make promises which they cannot keep. For instance they say they will reduce unemployment, but the number of people out of work remains static.

2

Every Roman town had at its centre a forum, where people came together to conduct their offical and religious affairs. In addition, the forum was used as a meeting place.

3

The meteorological office predicted rain for the two weeks of the Olympic Games. In consequence there were fewer spectators than we had anticipated.

4

Learning a foreign language can be difficult and at times frustrating. However the rewards usually outweigh the difficulties involved.

5

Not only did the Second World War result in the displacement of millions of innocent civilians, it also caused tremendous political change.

6

Despite the efforts of the government to reduce the incidence of smoking among teenagers and young adults, I regret to say that smoking is not in decline.

7

This is how to approach writing an essay. First, you should read the question carefully. Then you should make some notes covering your main ideas. After that you can start writing.

8

No matter how hard you try to justify the sport of fox hunting, the fact remains that animals are slaughtered simply to provide entertainment for humans.

9

Firstly I would like to talk about the early life of J.F. Kennedy. Secondly, we will look at the period of his presidency, and thirdly we will review the effects of his assassination.

10

On the one hand, it may be advisable to study hard the night before an exam; on the other hand, it is wise to get a good night's sleep before sitting a test.

UNIT 6, EXTRACT 2

TUTOR　OK, come on in. Hi Ben, hello Mark, Sally. Let's get going shall we, because we've got a lot of ground to cover this afternoon. It's Ben's turn to give his tutorial paper today but, remember, we do encourage questions from the rest of you, so do try to join in and ask questions.

BEN　OK.

TUTOR　Now, I believe Ben's going to talk to us today about the exploration of the Red Planet.

BEN　That's right. I'm going to be looking at the recent landing by the Americans of a spacecraft on the planet Mars and in particular focusing on the small rover robot.

MARK　Is that the little robot that *functions as a geologist*?

BEN　Yes, that's right. It's called a rover – like a land rover, I suppose! – and it can detect the geological composition of the ground it's standing on so, yes, *it's a sort of geologist*. It's actually quite amazing.

TUTOR　I heard it described as being *like a microwave oven on wheels*.

BEN　Yeah, well from an appearance point of view, that's a fair description. I've photocopied a picture of it for you, so that you can keep this for reference and make some notes and I'll just hand that out now.

VOICES　Thanks.

MARK　Wow, you'd actually expect it to look more space age than this, wouldn't you? Like more sophisticated.

BEN　OK, well as you can see it's quite small. It actually only weighs 16.5 kg.

TUTOR　Right, and what kind of speed is it capable of, Ben?

BEN　Um, well I suppose that depends on the terrain, but I understand that it has a top speed of 2.4 km an hour *which isn't very fast*, really.

TUTOR　And can you tell us how it works, explain some of these things we can see here?

BEN　Well first of all *on the top it's fitted with solar panels*. It runs on solar energy, of course.

SALLY　Does that mean it can't work at night?

BEN　Yes, indeed it does. I guess it sleeps at night! So you have the solar panels on the top, and *underneath this is the part known as the 'warm box'*.

MARK　What's the purpose of that?

BEN　Well, at night the temperatures on Mars can go below 100 degrees, so the warm box is designed to protect the electronics from the extreme cold. *It's also fitted with two cameras on the front*.

TUTOR　OK. And what about its wheels?

BEN　It's got *six aluminium wheels*, each 13 cm in diameter. Each one has its own motor, so it's individually powered, which allows the vehicle to turn on the spot if necessary. And as you know aluminium is very light.

MARK　And how is it steered?

BEN　Good question! It's steered using virtual reality goggles worn by someone back on earth, believe it or not, though because the robot can't be manipulated in real time it can't be steered in real time either.

SALLY　What do you mean exactly?

BEN　Well you see it takes more than 11 minutes for a radio signal to travel from command headquarters in California to Mars and another 11 minutes for the answer to come back.

SALLY　You mean *there's a time delay*.

BEN　Yes, exactly. And the time delay or time lag means it can't be steered directly from Earth. So what they do is this. They photograph the area around the rover and the scientists will decide where they want the rover to go.

TUTOR　In other words, *they'll plot a course for the rover*.

BEN　Exactly.

TUTOR　OK, Ben, that's very interesting. Now can you tell us anything about this space mission itself? Why Mars?

BEN   Well, people have been fascinated by Mars for a long time and it is generally believed that *Mars is the only other planet* in the solar system *to have abundant water.*

TUTOR Is it possible that people might one day be able to live on Mars?

BEN   Well of course there's a lot of work to be done yet, but theoretically I can't see why not.

TUTOR Thanks, Ben, that was very interesting.

UNIT 7, EXTRACT 2

LECTURER

Today, in our series of lectures on human language, **we are going to be looking** at the way in which children acquire language. The study of how people learn to speak has proved to be one of the most *fascinating, important and complex* branches of language study. **So let's look at these three features in turn. Firstly** – why is it fascinating? This stems from the *natural interest* people take in the developing abilities of young children. People are *fascinated* by the way in which children learn, particularly their own children!

Secondly, it is *important* to study how we acquire our first language, because the study of child language can lead us to a greater understanding of language as a whole. **The third** point is that it's a *complex* study and this is because of the enormous difficulties that are encountered by researchers as soon as they attempt to explain language development, especially in the very young child.

In today's lecture we will cover a number of topics. **We will start by** talking about *research methods*. There are a number of ways that researchers have investigated children's language and these include the use of diaries, recordings and tests, and we'll be looking at how researchers make use of these various *methods*. **We will then go on** to examine *the language learning process*, starting with the development of speech in young infants during the first year of life. This is the time associated with the emergence of the skills of speech perception, **in other words**, an emergence of the child's awareness of his or her own ability to speak. **We will continue** with our examination of *the language learning process*, **this time by** looking at language learning in the older child, that is in children under five. As they mature, it is possible to begin *analysis* in conventional linguistic terms, and **so** in our *analysis* **we will look at** phonological, grammatical and semantic development in pre-school children.

In the second part of the talk I would like to review some *educational approaches* to the question of how linguistic skills can be developed. **In other words**, how can we assist the young child to learn language skills at school? **Initially** we will look at issues that arise in relation to *spoken* language; we will **then** look at *reading* and review a number of approaches that have been proposed in relation to the *teaching of reading*. **Finally we will conclude** today's talk with an account of current thinking about the most neglected area of all, the child's developing *awareness of written language.*

UNIT 7, EXTRACT 3

LECTURER

In today's lecture I want to look at one of Australia's least loved animals, but one that has an interesting history from which, I think, we can learn a fundamental lesson about problem solving.

While Australia is famous for its many wonderful native animals, in particular the kangaroo and the koala, it also has some less attractive animals, many of which were actually brought to Australia in the 19th and 20th centuries.

Perhaps the most well known introduced animal is *the rabbit*, brought originally by the early settlers as a source of food. Another animal to be introduced by the settlers was the fox, for the purpose of *sport* in the form of *fox hunting*.

But perhaps the most unusual animal ever brought here was the cane toad. Here is a picture of one. (Picture at bottom of page) It is a large, and some people would say, very ugly species of toad and was deliberately imported to this country by *the sugar cane farmers* in 1935 to eradicate the beetle which kills the sugar cane plant.

The cane beetle is the natural enemy of the sugar cane plant. It lives in the cane and drops its eggs onto the ground around the base of the plant. The eggs develop into grubs and then *the grub eats the roots of the cane* resulting in *the death of the plant*. In the mid thirties there was a serious outbreak of cane beetle and the farmers became desperate to get rid of the pest which was ruining their livelihood.

Meanwhile news was trickling in from overseas about a toad, *native to central America* which supposedly ate the beetles which killed the cane. It was reported that the toad had been taken to Hawaii, where cane is also grown, and introduced with apparent success. So with the backing of the Queensland authorities, the farmers arranged to import one hundred toads from Hawaii. The toads were then released into the cane fields to undertake the eradication of the cane beetle.

As predicted the toads started to breed successfully and within a very short time *their numbers had swollen*. But there was one serious problem. It turned out that cane toads do not eat cane beetles. And the reason for this is that toads live on insects that are found on the ground and the cane beetle lives at the top of the cane plant well out of reach of the toads. In fact they never come into contact with each other.

Now you may well ask: How did this terrible mistake ever happen? And the reason is quite simply that the farmers were desperate to find a way of ridding their fields of the cane beetle and so *they accepted the reports that had been written without ever doing their own research*. And the added irony is that in 1947, just twelve years later, an effective pesticide was developed which kills the beetle, thereby *ensuring the survival of the sugar cane industry to this day*. Meanwhile much of tropical north east Australia is infested with the cane toad which serves no purpose whatsoever and experts claim that the toad is spreading south in plague proportions.

Now as agricultural scientists, we have to ask ourselves: what lessons are to be learned from this tale? And I can think of three main points. Firstly, one should never rely on claims which are not backed up by evidence, i.e. in this case, evidence that the cane toad actually eats the grub of the cane beetle and thereby kills the pest.

Secondly, *we should look very carefully at possible effects of introducing any living species into a new environment*, and lastly, one should not allow one's decision making to be influenced by a sense of desperation which may cloud the issue. In other words, one should always seek objective advice.

IELTS PRACTICE LISTENING TEST

SECTION 1

AGENT	Good morning.
STUDENT	Good morning. Um … I'm looking for a place to rent near the university.
AGENT	What are you after? A house, a flat … a room?
STUDENT	Well, *preferably a house*, if that's possible. There are three of us looking altogether. We thought we might share if we could find something suitable.
AGENT	So something near the university?
STUDENT	Yes, if that's at all possible. We're all students so it'd be good if we could find something *within walking distance of the campus*. None of us has a car and we don't want to have to take public transport.
AGENT	Yeah, well everybody wants that of course.
STUDENT	Yeah, I suppose they do.
AGENT	Are you in your first year?
STUDENT	No, I've been here a year already. Last year we all lived in a hall of residence. *That was really great*, even the food wasn't too bad. *We had a lot of fun there*. But in the second year they kick you out into the real world!

AGENT   OK, so let me have a look and see what we've got … Well, there's a two-bedroom house in Newtown which is quite cheap.

STUDENT   That'd be good because it's very near the university, but if we all want our own rooms *it isn't really big enough.*

AGENT   *Too small.* Give that one a miss?

STUDENT   Yeah, I think so. Got anything else?

AGENT   What about this? Three-bedroom flat, close to the university. … *It's $400 a week.*

STUDENT   Oh, *that's too expensive.*

AGENT   Alright, well … here's something that might interest you. It's a three-bedroom house with garden.

STUDENT   Not bothered about the garden, but where is it?

AGENT   Near the airport.

STUDENT   That's miles from the university.

AGENT   Yes, it is quite far, but *it's reasonably priced at $250.00 a week.* Why don't you go and have a look?

STUDENT   Oh … alright. We will. Can I have the address?

AGENT   Right, well it's at *14a Station Road,* Botany.

STUDENT   Is anyone living there at the moment?

AGENT   No, it's vacant.

STUDENT   And does it have any furniture?

AGENT   Well it says here that it's partially furnished.

STUDENT   What does that mean exactly?

AGENT   Well there's a kitchen table and chairs, two single beds, *a double bed,* two wardrobes, a kitchen cooker and *a washing machine.* Not bad really for the money.

STUDENT   Is there a fridge?

AGENT   It doesn't mention it here. I can let you have the key and you can pop round and see for yourself.

STUDENT   Right … thanks. We'll do that.

AGENT   Hello … you're back. How did you find the house?

STUDENT   Well … not bad. It's certainly large enough and there's quite a big garden, but *it's completely overgrown.* You can hardly get out the back door because the grass is so high. *We'd have to have it tidied up* a bit before we moved in.

AGENT   OK.

STUDENT   The kitchen is fine, but there's an awful smell throughout the house.

AGENT   The place hasn't been occupied for a couple of months, so that's probably why it's a bit musty. It'll be fine when you open up the windows and let some fresh air in.

STUDENT   Yeah, well I think *the landlord ought to pay to clean the carpets* at least.

AGENT   I can put that to him, though I'm not sure whether he'll agree. We can but ask.

STUDENT   OK. Well if he does, we'd probably be interested …

SECTION 2

PRESENTER
Hello and welcome to *Cooking Capers.* And this week we're looking at that most versatile and aromatic of plants: a fairly recent addition to the list of Australian agricultural produce, but nevertheless, a great favourite today – ginger. And in the studio to tell us all about it is Monica Maxwell.

MONICA
Ginger is one of my personal favourite spices and I've got a number of wonderful recipes to share with you later on in the programme. So what is ginger? Well, actually it's a spicy-tasting root with an aromatic flavour; *it's related to the bamboo family* and has a hundred different uses in the kitchen. The Chinese have cultivated it for years, *particularly to use in medicine,* though you are probably more familiar with its culinary uses. But first, let's take a brief look at its history before we look at how it can be used, because it's had a very interesting history. Ginger *originated in the southern provinces of China and in India,* where it had been used in medicines and food preparation for over 5000 years. The early traders who came upon the plant took it to many parts of the world such as Nigeria, the West Indies, Central America, East Africa and even Indonesia.

Ginger became extremely popular because of its exotic, aromatic properties and was highly valued by spice traders in the 17th and 18th centuries because *they were able to sell it back in Europe for a very good price.* Although Australia is now the largest producer of ginger in the world, *it wasn't grown in Australia until the early 20th century.*

Apparently some pieces of raw ginger found their way to an area about 100 km north of Brisbane in Queensland earlier this century. The comparatively *high rainfall and humidity* in this area *produce conditions which are perfect for growing ginger.* So it became well established, but in the early days *the relatively high cost of production placed it at a disadvantage in the market* by comparison with the much cheaper ginger produced by other countries with lower production costs.

Then in 1941 the supply of ginger to Australia started to run out. Remember … *this was in the middle of the Second World War* when everything was in short supply. This provided the perfect opportunity for the Queensland growers to expand their production and sales. Five local farmers got together and formed a cooperative association in a place called Buderim. They started with only *25 pounds* between them. (That was in the days when Australian currency was pounds, not dollars.)

So they set up the company with two wooden vats and *14 tons of raw ginger*, but they went on to become the most successful ginger farmers in the world.

In fact nearly all the world's ginger now comes from the Buderim ginger factory in Queensland. *40% of the production is used in Australia* and the remaining 60% is exported overseas to places like Europe, North America, South Africa, and even to Asia, where it originated in the first place.

So now let's move on to looking at ways of using ginger in the kitchen …

SECTION 3

INTERVIEWER Dr Clarke, global warming was the threat of the 1980s but it seems to have fizzled out of people's minds – why do you think that is?

DR CLARKE Yes, in a way you're right. I think scientists have become occupied with the task of trying to find out whether it really is happening and, if so, *whether it's caused by human activity.*

INTERVIEWER A greenhouse effect is, after all, a natural phenomenon …

DR CLARKE Yes, as we know, naturally occurring gases float above us, acting as insulators that prevent heat being radiated into space.

INTERVIEWER And the fear is that the insulation might get thicker …

DR CLARKE Yes … and *because of this, the earth might get warmer.*

INTERVIEWER The latest prediction we've heard is that temperature will increase by about a third of a degree every ten years. What are your feelings?

DR CLARKE Well … this prediction is difficult to make. You see the global climate is the result of *a web of influences.* Who is to say that a simple action such as adding carbon dioxide to the atmosphere will not have several effects which might even cancel each other out?

INTERVIEWER And I understand that the prediction is hard to verify whatever …

DR CLARKE Precisely.

INTERVIEWER Why is that?

DR CLARKE Because *the earth's temperature surges and subsides naturally.* In fact the best way of detecting global temperature change is to measure the temperature of the oceans as accurately as possible.

INTERVIEWER And this avoids the sort of seasonal fluctuations of the temperature of land mass.

DR CLARKE   Yes – in fact *an understanding of the oceans is crucial to understanding how the global climate works.* The ocean transports heat around the globe. It's like a great reservoir of heat – a tiny change in sea surface temperature denotes a huge change in the amount of heat it is storing.

INTERVIEWER   And now, I understand you are looking at ways of refining this measurement of ocean temperature.

DR CLARKE   Yes. For a long time, we've measured it by placing thermometers in buoys bobbing in the oceans and also *when ships draw water through their engines.*

INTERVIEWER   It's also been done by satellite, hasn't it?

DR CLARKE   Yes. But now data from a more promising system is being collected. This is the European along-track scanning radiometer or ATSR, a much simpler name. The ATSR *orbits the earth above us.*

INTERVIEWER   And what stage are you at with this?

DR CLARKE   Well it's been up there two and a half years now. It's an infra-red detector that senses *the earth's temperature with great accuracy* and this is what we need … we have to be able to separate out random changes in temperature.

INTERVIEWER   I believe there are other advantages as well?

DR CLARKE   There are several … Every few days *it covers the entire earth. So it produces large quantities of data.* It measures the temperature from two angles, which allows correction for any effects that the intervening atmosphere may be having on its readings. *Its field of view has a width of 500 km* and it measures the temperature to 0.3 degrees centigrade.

INTERVIEWER   And it should go on for years?

DR CLARKE   Yes.

INTERVIEWER   Thank you, Dr Clarke, for talking to us today … and now over to …

SECTION 4

PRESENTER

Well, we're delighted to have the opportunity to hear from Sue Gent, our specialist on student affairs, about a course with a difference.

SUE GENT

Thank you, Tony.

'Many people think that conservation is just about saving fluffy animals – what they don't realise is that it is a war, to save the human race from committing suicide.' Strong words – but this was the belief of the famous conservationist – Gerald Durrell.

Gerald Durrell was an English conservationist who dedicated his life to the conservation of animals, and among his many achievements was the establishment of a zoo in Jersey. There he set up the Wildlife Preservation Trust, which conducts courses on preservation and attracts *students from developing countries*; many of these students are making their first trip away from home.

The students who come to Jersey to study are of all ages. The first was a man called Jousseff Mungroo, who came from Mauritius in 1977. *He was particularly interested in the conservation of large African birds.* When he arrived, there were only four Mauritius falcons – these are big birds of prey – left in his African homeland. Now, since he has returned, the numbers have increased to 200. When Jousseff first arrived in Jersey he was unused to the freezing winters, *so he liked to spend time in the reptile house.* He said it was the warmest place on the island!

So let's look at how students are chosen to participate in one of the zoo's programmes. Well, according to their teacher *their work or study must involve animals* – the zoo is proud of the fact that many of its graduates are now in positions to influence the way animals are kept and utilised for conservation. Once they start the course, the students have to spend a lot of time *studying the English language*, in addition to that they also have *to cover many aspects of animal conservation.*

This year 27 students from 21 different countries are already waiting to participate in the intensive training programmes at the zoo. In a principles and practice course they learn both theory and practice: first they learn the theory of conservation biology, working in areas such as veterinary medicine. Then they move into the practical part of the course and *work with the zoo keepers*, where they learn to care for the animals.

Over 350 full-time students have graduated since Jousseff Mungroo, and, like him, some graduates have made big names for themselves in the zoo and conservation world. *A former Chinese student* is now responsible for captive breeding and conservation throughout his country and a student from Mauritius who trained at the zoo is the present *Conservation Officer* for Mauritius.

Answer Key

Listening Unit 1

Extract 1

Who?	Why? *Suggested answers*
1 Waiter/customer	Taking the order in a restaurant
2 Policeman/driver	Man was speeding
3 Husband/wife	Telling wife about the fine
4 Lecturer	Giving a lecture/talk
5 Student/sports club clerk	Seeking information on joining club
6 Student/lecturer or tutor	Asking for an extension
7 Student/student	Discussing an assignment
8 Flight attendant/passenger	Offering a drink
9 Doctor/patient	Consultation: patient describing his/her problem
10 College principal to students	Welcome speech

Discussion questions

11 Unprepared speech contains hesitations, repetition and redundancy. Language written to be read out loud is dense and may contain a lot of information and complex grammatical structures. Speech is often easier to understand because it contains repetition and hesitation.

12 Spoken language is usually face to face – facial expression and gesture and context help you to understand. On the telephone you do not have this help because you cannot see the other speaker. Recorded conversations are similar because you are not part of the conversation yourself. You are an 'outsider'. When listening to an IELTS recording, you need to make good use of any clues included in the question or in the sound effects on the tape.

Listening Unit 2

Extract 1

1 Friday (night)
2 7.30
3 Video recorder // VCR
4 £50
5 (University) bookshop
6 not available // out of print
7 (new) football boots
8 12.00
9 (the) flu
10 Mon(day), 3.30 (pm)
11 (some/a pair of/Mr Lee's) glasses
12 customer service desk
13 (farewell) party
14 9818 4078

Extract 2

1 Coffee
2 9.30(am)
3 (free) (souvenir) postcard
4 $42
5 (3-course) lunch
6 2.15 (pm)
7 sandwiches
8 opposite (the) shops
9 English (only)
10 wear/take a hat

Extract 3

1 Frank Moorcroft
2 19 Lake Road
3 3697 4500
4 UT 9128
5 23 June (not *tomorrow*)
6 C
7 C
8 B
9 A
10 B

Listening Unit 3

Extract 1

1 A
2 C
3 C
4 B
5 A
6 A

Listening Unit 4

Extract 1

The reason it is not always possible to predict what people are going to say is that, by definition, every utterance is an original one. Whereas, for example, the predictable conversation between a librarian and student would be about a book, we could not predict the possibility that one was inviting the other out for dinner. The following examples are, however, all of a predictable nature.

NB The answers in the last two columns are only examples, out of many possible answers. What is important is that you have *understood* the topic and how it develops.

	Situation	Introductory phrase	Topic?	How does the topic develop?
1	Department store: customer and sales assistant	Can I help you?	Returning a tie	Tie can't be changed
2	Husband and wife talking about the children	You know, John	Maria's school work	Father agrees to speak to daughter
3	Radio news item	And now, closer to home …	Hospital waiting lists	Length of time people wait for surgery
4	Two friends making plans for an outing	Now, about this (picnic)	Where to have picnic	Agreement reached on where to go
5	Two students chatting in university canteen	You know the (assignment)	Concerns about an assignment	Agreement reached on what course of action to take
6	University librarian and student	Excuse me	Finding a book in the library	Solution: to buy own copy
7	Sports equipment shop: assistant and two teenagers	Hey! You guys!	Telling customers to behave	Rude exchange of words
8	Vice Chancellor of a university speaking at a ceremony	Good afternoon …	Welcome to graduation ceremony	Importance of the occasion

Extract 2

1 A
2 C
3 B
4 B
5 C
6 national interest//the country//the nation
7 living people
8 (past) kings and queens
9 C
10 B

Listening Unit 5

Pre-listening

a <u>I</u> thought the assignment was due in on Thursday. *What did you think?*
b I thought the <u>assignment</u> was due in on Thursday. *Now, I find it's the <u>exam</u> on Thursday.*
c I thought the assignment was due in on <u>Thursday</u>. *But it was due on Wednesday.*

Extract 1

1 No. Speed of delivery (i.e. he is speaking quickly). Falling intonation.
2 Yes. Hesitations and lack of interest in voice.
3 No. Customer's sarcastic tone, use of formal words.
4 Yes. Indirect answer – avoidance.
5 No. Lack of interest. Her flat tone – use of irony.
6 No. Mother's flat response and use of irony.
7 Yes. Negative question tag inviting agreement. Upward intonation.
8 No. The man's irritation and sarcastic tone.

Extract 2

1 B
2 C
3 D
4 A
5 C
6 C
7 B
8 D

Supplementary activity

I beg your pardon! = Please take back what you said, I don't agree with you
Oh, Frank, you know what I mean! = Don't be so annoying
from the cradle to the grave = from birth to death i.e. throughout your life
the party's over = the good times have come to an end; the money has run out
pushing back the frontiers of science = doing original scientific work
to get away from it all = to get away from the crowds, to find somewhere quiet to live
to have a roof over their heads = to have somewhere to live

Listening Unit 6

Extract 1

Here are some example answers, out of many possible answers.

1 … they say they will reduce unemployment, but the number of people out of work remains static.
2 … was used as a meeting place.
3 … there were fewer spectators than we had anticipated.
4 … the rewards usually outweigh the difficulties involved.
5 … also caused tremendous political change.
6 … is not in decline.
7 … you should make some notes covering your main ideas. After that you can start writing.
8 … animals are slaughtered simply to provide entertainment for humans.
9 … we will look at the period of his presidency and thirdly we will review the effects of his assassination.
10 … it is wise to get a good night's sleep before sitting a test.

Extract 2

1 geologist
2 microwave (oven)
3 slowly
4 solar panels
5 warm box
6 two cameras
7 aluminium
8 time lag/delay
9 course//journey
10 (plenty of/abundant) water

Listening Unit 7

Extract 2

1 interest
2 important
3 complex
4 research methods
5 (language) learning process
6 analysis
7 educational approaches
8 spoken
9 reading
10 writing // written language

Extract 3

1 rabbit
2 (fox) hunting // sport
3 sugar cane farmers
4 root of (sugar) cane
5 dies
6 A
7 B
8 C
9 A
10 C

Reading Unit 1

1 The IELTS Reading test.
2 To give information on the test.
3 Students who wish to sit IELTS.
4 To find out about the test.
5 Descriptive.
6 Geography/The Antarctic/Map-making (cartography).
7 Geography students.
8 Reasons why Antarctica is difficult to map.
9 To compare map-making in the Antarctic with the rest of the world.
10 The last sentence.

11 He has contributed to a report on soil.
12 By discussing some of the 'effects'.
13 It will present argument backed up by research, whereas 'The Dynamic Continent' is largely descriptive.
14 It separates main ideas.
15 The main ideas/topic sentences.
16 A
17 C

Reading Unit 2

1 concrete and glass
2 (the/its) diameter
3 (its) age and origin
4 by (a) volcano/volcanic eruption
5 (in) northern Scotland
6 geologists
7 Q4 because you can scan the text for the name.
8 Q6 because it refers to an argument.
9 hydraulic lift
10 lantern // beacon
11 34 miles
12 (up to) 300 rooms
13 circular storey
14 ✗
15 ✓
16 ✓
17 ✗
18 play (with it/them/the bears)
19 sleep (with it/them/the bears)

Reading Unit 3

1 C
2 A errors, maps
  B difficulties, reaching areas
  C changes
  D regularity, visit
3 Libraries are making digital copies of books. // Technology is going to change the way libraries work.
4 Paragraphs 2, 3 and 4
5 *three, First, for example, similarly*
6 Very easy, because the text is organised around the three benefits.
7 A ⎤ in
8 C ⎬ any
9 E ⎦ order
10 genes
11 barriers
12 droughts
13 irrigation

Supplementary activity

14 abandoned
15 crops
16 10m hectares
17 store
18 8/eight harvests

Reading Unit 4

1 ix
2 i
3 v
4 ii
5 vi
6 viii
7 iv
8 B

Reading Unit 5

1 preserved
2 responding
3 safe
4 modern
5 single
6 unsuccessful
7 significant
8 careful

Supplementary activity

9 E
10 B
11 A
12 C
13 E

Reading Unit 6

1 To discuss new research findings.
2 They conflict.
3 No firm conclusions are drawn.
4 Are humans a threat to penguins? New research says 'no'.
5 A ⎫ in
6 C ⎬ any
7 D ⎭ order
8 HA
9 SM
10 NC
11 RH
12 JA
13 NC
14 DG
15 MP

Supplementary activity

Suggested answers – just one example from many possible answers

16 Computers raise serious copyright issues, particularly for authors.
17 Scientists find it immensely difficult to understand why we dream, because the brain itself is extremely complicated.
18 Since we have little understanding of soils we must take care to allow them to recover after we use them, so as not to cause permanent damage.

Reading Unit 7

1a Fact. Even if we do not agree with the statement, it is presented as a fact.
 b Opinion, indicated by the words 'I find'.
 c Claim, because it is backed up by evidence.
 d The first part of the sentence (Many companies have schemes that reward high sales) is a fact. The second part of the sentence is an opinion, indicated by the words 'in my experience'.
 e Claim, indicated by the words 'say researchers in Britain'.
2 D
3 YES
4 NO
5 NOT GIVEN
6 NO
7 NOT GIVEN
8 YES
9 YES
10 *Suggested answers – just one example from many possible answers*
 a The writer feels that Dr Masson's point is diminished because he identifies too closely with the animals.
 b As a child, the writer had found his grandmother intimidating.
 c We do not question our views on animals' emotions sufficiently.
11 C
12 B
13 A

Supplementary activity

14 anxiety // difficulty
15 novelists // the novelist // the writer of fiction

16 channel of information
17 rewriting // revision
18 control over/of
19 right // opportunity
20 their/the director(s)

Reading Unit 8

1 Three.
2 1 hour.
3 40.
4 About 20 minutes.
5 'Social situations'.
6 C
7 D
8 A
9 B
10 TRUE
11 FALSE
12 TRUE
13 NOT GIVEN
14 C
15 D
16 B
17 E
18 A
19 E
20 F

Reading Unit 9

1 Course-related situations.
2 750 maximum.
3 Student accommodation.
4 One – Sturtin Hostel.
5 567233
6 876333
7 322756
8 223300
9 567233
10 ii
11 v
12 i
13 vii
14 viii

Supplementary activity

15 Sturtin Hostel
16 Highdown House
17 First Stop
18 Three Seasons
19 Downtown Digs

Writing Unit 1

Suggested answers

1 … an equal amount of money on entertainment and clothes.
2 … but she only spends 25% of her money on study materials.
3 … less on clothes than she spends …
4 … almost as much …
5 43% of//Just under half of
6 used to smoke
7 (relatively) small percentage/minority
8 heavier smokers
9 The percentage (NOT 'number')
10 are similar/are close to 11%

Writing Unit 2

1 The rise/growth in the number of overseas students at a university over a twenty-year period.
2 The number of overseas students studying at the university has risen considerably.
The graph shows a considerable increase in …
It gives a *more accurate* description.
3b a steady rise/a gradual increase
c a stable/constant pattern
d a peak
e a dramatic increase/a sharp rise
f a gradual decrease/fall
4b … rises steadily
c … remains constant
d … reaches a peak
e … increases dramatically/rises sharply
f … falls/decreases gradually
5 People (car owners).
6 Years.
7 Car owners in millions.
8 Car ownership in Britain has risen dramatically.
9a … has risen …
b … rose …
10a Since 1960, the number of car owners in Britain has risen dramatically from below 2 million to 25 million.
b The number of car owners in Britain rose dramatically from under 2 million in 1960 to 25 million in 2000.
11 Between 1980 and 1998, the number of students at the University rose considerably from just over 200 to 900.

12a The first graph shows the number of grocery stores that closed in Britain (in thousands) between 1961 and 1995. Between 1961 and 1971 there was a steep fall in the number of grocery stores closing in Britain and then a gradual fall until 1980. Very few stores closed between then and 1995.

12b The second graph shows the increase in the types of products sold at supermarkets between 1950 and 1995. The types of products stocked increased significantly from 550 to 19000 between 1950 and 1995.

12c The third graph shows the growth of supermarkets in Britain between 1985 and 1996.
During this time there was a steady growth in the number of supermarkets from 400 to 1000.

13 The number of hamburgers sold at Harry's over a one-year period.

14 The pattern is variable.

15 To get a clear picture of the trend in sales over the year.

16 The simple past tense.

17 *Suggested answers*

a The sale of hamburgers was stable through-out January, February and most of March.

b Fewer hamburgers were sold in April than in March according to this graph.

c There was a dramatic rise in the sale of hamburgers between June and August when numbers increased from 1900 to 3000.

d Hamburger sales peaked in August when 3000 were sold.

e The lowest sales of hamburgers were in October when they dropped to 1250 for the month.

f Hamburgers were more popular in summer than in winter according to this graph.

Model answer for the Follow-up activity on page 72

The graph shows the fluctuation in the number of people at a London underground station over the course of a day. According to the graph there is a sharp increase between 6.00 and 8.00 in the morning, with 400 people using the station at 8 o'clock. After this, the numbers fall dramatically to less than 200 at 10 o'clock. Between 11.00 and 3.00 the number of people rises and falls evenly with a plateau around lunchtime of just under 300 people using the station. Numbers then decline, with the lowest number being recorded at 4.00 in the afternoon. There is then a rapid rise between 4.00 and 6 pm during the evening rush hour with a peak of 380 people at 6 pm. After 7 pm numbers fall significantly, with only a slight increase again just after 8 pm, tailing off after 9 pm. The graph shows that the station is most crowded in the early morning and early evening rush-hour periods.

Writing Unit 3

Suggested answers

1 The graph shows the increase in the number of mobile phone owners in Europe between 1995 and 2000.

2 Overall, the number of (mobile phone) owners has risen considerably since 1995. In some countries the figure has more than doubled over the five years.

3 In France, for example, the number of (mobile phone) owners has increased sevenfold from one million in 1995 to seven million in 2000.

4 In 1995, the UK had the greatest number of owners at just under five million and this figure increased to 12 million in 2000.

5 The greatest number of mobile phone owners is now in Germany, where ownership has risen from four million in 1995 to 14 million in 2000.

6 faster/better/more successful than

7 narrowest/smallest

8 while/whereas

9 less

10 difference

Writing Unit 4

1 *Suggested answer – some words and phrases have been italicised for discussion.*
The diagram illustrates how a new dredging boat will be used in the future to drain canals in Venice of mud.
The boat will carry a suction pump *with* rotating blades on the end of it *which* will be lowered into the canal by two hydraulic arms. *These rotating blades* will stir up the mud, called slurry, on the bottom of the canal *and this* will *then* be sucked up by the centrifugal pump. *From the pump*, the mud will be discharged *through* a large tube into a shuttle boat *located* behind the

dredging boat. *When the shuttle boat* is full of mud, it will be towed out of the city *and* the mud will be dumped.

Writing Unit 5

1 *explaining, tell, ask*
2 What you, as the writer, wish to express, e.g. a suggestion, a complaint, an invitation, a request, an apology *plus* the desired outcome.
3 Poor style, rambling, not getting to the point, not stating your purpose clearly, being rude or offensive.
4 To complain and get a refund or similar recompense.
5 Formal, polite.
6 Less formally and possibly without reference initially to the purpose of the letter e.g. 'I've been meaning to write to you …' or simply 'I'm terribly sorry …'.

Example answers
7 I am writing with reference to the bill you sent me …
8 I hope you're not busy on …
9 I have applied for a new job and I wonder if you would be kind enough to …
10 I recently paid you $400 to do some repair work on my car.

Writing Unit 6

1 Disappointment, anger, surprise, shock, etc.
2 They are rather informal, very direct and many of them would seem offensive or rude.
3 They might be offended and react in a hostile or uncooperative way.

A model answer to GT Writing Task 1 is given on page 186.

Writing Unit 7

1 At least 250.
2 About 40 minutes.
3 Argumentative/discursive/descriptive.
4 Reasons (GT); examples and evidence (Academic).
5 Good organisation, clear ideas that directly address the topic, coherent argument, accurate and appropriate structures and vocabulary, good punctuation and spelling.
6 **a** possible; **c**; **e** possible; **f** possible; **g**; **i**

Writing Unit 8

1 The writer should be able to follow the development of the argument throughout the answer.
2 Selecting main ideas and developing support.
3 Some will be expanded, some will be discarded.
4 The main areas/ideas to be developed. (This is why the introduction does not come first in this unit.)
5 Roughly a fifth of the answer, i.e. 30–60 words – keep a balance with other parts.
6 Five minutes.
7 By starting a new paragraph.
8 *What is meant by …*
   How can you judge …
   How do you measure …
9 *Generally, I agree with the argument that …*
   I tend to disagree …
   I am unconvinced by …
10 *Example answer*
   It has been argued that if you treat all staff at work equally, you will improve the success of your company. But how can you make every employee feel valued and will this really make a company more successful? By addressing these questions, I intend to show that this argument is unrealistic and makes too many assumptions about human behaviour.
11 30–50 words – conclusions are often shorter than introductions because our ideas can be summed up quite easily, although this doesn't have to be the case.
12 By starting a new paragraph.

A model answer to the writing task on the topic of immunisation is given on page 185.

Writing Unit 9

1 Very strong – NB use of *convinced, essential, largely, overall, only*
2 By looking at positive approaches to examinations.
   By examining the benefits of examinations.

Supplementary activity

Suggested answers

3 in favour of
4 In other words/In this way
5 I would argue that/Certainly
6 Admittedly/In some ways
7 honestly don't think/doubt
8 think/believe (that)
9 Surely/Arguably/Either way/In any case

Writing Unit 10

1 No.
2 It lacks coherence. It's rather chatty. There is a mix of arguments with little support.
3 Something like: In the past neighbourhoods were often very close, friendly places whereas in today's society people have little time to get to know each other. How does this affect our sense of belonging to a community?
4 Main argument – good neighbour relations are advantageous
Supporting argument – examples of good and poor relations today
5 Examples and personal experience.
6 for example/instance; If this is the case
7 In fact/Indeed; Of course/Naturally
8 In my experience
9 for example/in fact/indeed

Supplementary activity

A model answer to GT Writing Task 2 is given on page 186.

Writing Unit 11

1 This drop/fall
2 These figures
3 these/such qualities

Suggested answer

There is always some controversy over whether it is important to spend large sums of money on medical research <u>or</u> whether more of this money should be directed towards treating patients. <u>Obviously</u> some medical research is essential. <u>Without it</u>, we would have no vaccinations against diseases <u>such as</u> polio, no drugs <u>such as</u> antibiotics and no treatments <u>like</u> x-rays or radiotherapy. <u>Nevertheless</u>, the field of medical research is very competitive <u>and</u> <u>this</u> has financial disadvantages. <u>Take, for example</u>, the current research being conducted on the HIV virus. <u>In this field</u> it is arguable that money is being wasted <u>in that</u> scientists throughout the world are working independently towards the same ultimate goal – to find a cure for AIDS – <u>and</u> with the same hope of becoming famous in the process. <u>Surely</u> it would be more productive <u>and</u> less costly if <u>these scientists</u> joined forces <u>and</u> an international research team was set up <u>with</u> joint international funding.

5 The graph shows that the number of students in higher education in the UK has risen over the past five years.
6 40 per cent of students said they expected to earn around £21,000 when they start work, while only 2 per cent expected a salary of £40,000 or more.
7 A typical British town has a population of 180,000 and a police force of 2500 officers, yet (of these) there are only 10 officers patrolling the streets at any one time.
8 Drink-driving laws vary from country to country; for example, in Poland it is illegal to drive with more than 20 mg of alcohol in your blood, while in Italy the figure is 80 mg.
9 In France, the percentage of one-person households has risen over the past 10 years from 27 per cent in 1989 to 30 per cent in 1999.
10 55,000 students enrolled in the Biological Sciences this year, which is an increase (over last year) of nine per cent and marks the biggest change in the enrolment of students in first-degree courses.

Suggested answer

11 A sample of one hundred people were interviewed at random about their views on the Internet. While the majority of those interviewed had heard of the computer facility, relatively few knew how to use it and only 20 per cent of the sample had access to it. In most cases, those who said they could use the Internet were students or were, not surprisingly, under 40 years of age. The minority who had not even heard of it tended to be 60 years old or more. Overall it was felt that the sample was representative of the general population.

Writing Unit 8 Academic Writing Task 2 Model Answers – Opposing points of view

Should parents be obliged to immunise their children against common childhood diseases? Or do individuals have the right to choose not to immunise their children?

Band 9 answer

Some people argue that the state does not have the right to make parents immunise their children. However, I feel the question is not whether they should immunise but whether, as members of society, they have the right not to.

Introduction restates the question posed in the task.
Definitive statement clarifying the writer's opinion, with examples.

Preventative medicine has proved to be the most effective way of reducing the incidence of fatal childhood diseases. As a result of the widespread practice of immunising young children in our society, many lives have been saved and the diseases have been reduced to almost zero.

In previous centuries children died from ordinary illnesses such as influenza and tuberculosis and because few people had immunity, the diseases spread easily. Diseases such as dysentery were the result of poor hygiene but these have long been eradicated since the arrival of good sanitation and clean water. Nobody would suggest that we should reverse this good practice now because dysentery has been wiped out.

Comparison with historical background to support argument. Supporting argument with examples.

Serious diseases such as polio and smallpox have also been eradicated through national immunisation programmes. In consequence, children not immunised are far less at risk in this disease-free society than they would otherwise be. Parents choosing not to immunise are relying on the fact that the diseases have already been eradicated. If the number of parents choosing not to immunise increased, there would be a similar increase in the risk of the diseases returning.

Supporting evidence for argument in favour of immunisation with examples.

Immunisation is not an issue like seatbelts which affects only the individual. A decision not to immunise will have widespread repercussions for the whole of society and for this reason, I do not believe that individuals have the right to stand aside. In my opinion immunisation should be obligatory.

Conclusion and statement of personal opinion.

274 words

Band 9 answer

The issue of whether we should force parents to immunise their children against common diseases is, in my opinion, a social rather than a medical question. Since we are free to choose what we expose our bodies to in the way of food, drink, or religion for that matter, why should the question of medical 'treatment' be any different?

Introduction – poses a new question to introduce the topic.

Medical researchers and governments are primarily interested in overall statistics and trends and in money-saving schemes which fail to take into consideration the individual's concerns and rights. While immunisation against diseases such as tetanus and whooping cough may be effective, little information is released about the harmful effects of vaccinations which can sometimes result in stunted growth or even death.

Main argument

Concessional argument in support with example

The body is designed to resist disease and to create its own natural immunity through contact with that disease. So when children are given artificial immunity, we create a vulnerable society which is entirely dependent on immunisation. In the event that mass immunisation programmes were to cease, the society as a whole would be more at risk than ever before.

Writer's opinion stated plainly and forcefully – as fact.

In addition there is the issue of the rights of the individual. As members of a society, why should we be obliged to subject our children to this potentially harmful practice? Some people may also be against immunisation on religious grounds and their needs must also be considered.

Main idea with supporting arguments

For these reasons I feel strongly that immunisation programmes should not be obligatory and that the individual should have the right to choose whether or not to participate.

Personal opinion to sum up. Restatement of original question in own words.
252 words

Writing Unit 6 Model answer for GT Writing Task 1

You have a friend who lives in a city abroad. You have decided that you would like to apply to do a course at one of the colleges in this city. Write to your friend explaining what you would like to do. Tell him/her what type of work or studies you have been doing for the past few years and ask for assistance in contacting an appropriate institution.

Band 9 answer

Dear Anita

Sorry I haven't written for ages. I've been so busy over the last year and I never seem to have a minute to myself.

Informal introduction

I'd like to study electrical engineering at university in Australia next year and I hope you can give me some advice. I think I would prefer Melbourne because I know a few people from my visit last year.

Purpose of letter. Inclusion of some original information.

This year I'm doing maths and physics at school and I hope to do well in my exams. However, I really don't know which university to apply to, so could you send me some information about different colleges? Also can you find out what qualifications I need? For instance, as an overseas student, do I have to take an English test?

Answers the second part of the task, giving background information to the situation.

Poses a new question and answers the third part of the task.

I hope you don't mind doing this for me. It is much better to get this information from someone who lives in the country, so I hope to hear from you soon.

Closing paragraph – repeats the request in anticipation of a response.

Many thanks,

Rosanna

161 words

Writing Unit 10 Model answer for Supplementary activity, GT Writing Task 2

Disruptive school students have a negative influence on others. Students who are noisy and disobedient should be grouped together and taught separately. Do you agree or disagree? Give reasons for your answer.

Band 9 answer

There is no doubt that some students in schools behave badly and their behaviour causes difficulty for others either because it has a negative effect on the group or because ordinary students find it difficult to study with them.

First paragraph agrees in part with the proposition in the question and builds on it to form an introduction.

One solution is to take these students away and teach them on their own. However, if we simply have them removed after one or two warnings, we are limiting their educational opportunities because it seems to me that a school which caters for difficult students is a sort of "prison" whatever name you give it and the people who go there may never recover from the experience. This can then cause problems for the wider society.

Second paragraph outlines a problem arising from the solution offered in the question and poses a new problem.

Perhaps we need to look at why the disruptive students behave badly before we separate them. Disruptive students may be very intelligent and find the classes boring because the work is too easy. Perhaps these students need extra lessons rather than separate lessons. Or perhaps the teachers are uninspiring and this results in behavioural problems so we need better teachers. On the other hand, most students put up with this situation rather than cause trouble, and some people argue that we have to learn to suffer bad teachers and boring situations and that students who can't learn this lesson need to be taught separately.

Third paragraph looks at possible reasons why students may behave badly and suggests other solutions from the one in the question.

A counter argument is put forward for balance.

So before we condemn the students to a special school, we should look at factors such as the teaching, because once the children have been separated, it is very unlikely that they will be brought back.

Fourth paragraph sums up the suggestions in third paragraph and suggests further investigation.

255 words

Speaking Unit 1

More practice for part 1

Sample answers – others may be possible

1 It is very important for me to learn English because I want to get an interesting job in the tourist industry and it'll be much easier if I have good English.
2 I work as a bank teller in a bank, which can be a bit boring as many people do their banking by telephone or on the Internet now.
3 Tennis is a wonderful game, but you have to be very determined to play it well. I enjoy playing tennis as well as watching it.
4 At the moment I live in a very small apartment, but I would like to have a larger one. Hopefully I will, one day.
5 Take-away food is very popular in many countries these days even though it is bad for our health. I think cooking at home is more sensible because take-away food is expensive.
6 It was impossible to know everyone at my school because it was very large, and there were hundreds of children. I didn't even know all the teachers.
7 I love movies and I like watching TV. But I don't like live theatre, or opera either.
8 I swim to keep fit, which I think is very important, especially while I'm studying. Unless you work to keep fit, you run the risk of getting ill, and it's very difficult to study if you're not well.

Speaking Unit 2

Explaining how you feel – now and then

Sample answers – others may be possible
The reason why I enjoy eating out is that you don't have to do any washing up.
One of the good things about working from home is being able to organise your time as you like.
One of the bad things about living in the city centre is not being able to park your car very easily.
One of the problems with working abroad is that you can't see your family as often as you'd like to.

Giving short answers to the follow-up questions

1 Yes, there were. /No, there weren't. Yes, I think there were. /No, I don't think there were.
2 Yes, it is. /No, it isn't. Yes, I think it is. /No, I don't think it is.
3 Yes, I am. /No, I'm not. Yes, I think I am. /No, I don't think I am.
4 Yes, I did. /No, I didn't. Yes, I think I did. /No, I don't think I did.
5 Yes, I had. /No, I hadn't.
6 Yes, I will. /No, I won't. Yes, I think I will. / No, I don't think I will.
7 Yes, I can. /No, I can't.
8 Yes, I am. /No, I'm not. Yes, I think I am. /No, I don't think I am.

Speaking Unit 3

Links to the sub-theme

1 Work and Housing
2 Architecture
3 Work and Housing
4 The role of the State
5 Architecture
6 The role of the State
7 Architecture

Practice Test

Listening Section 1

1 B
2 A
3 not big enough // too small
4 too expensive // $400 a week
5 reasonably priced // $250 a week // cheap
6 14a Station Road
7 C/E
8 E/C
9 B/D
10 D/B

Listening Section 2

11 medicine // medicinal purposes
12 China AND India
13 a good price/(a) lot of money
14 (early) 20th century
15 perfect/ideal (conditions)

16 production cost(s) // cost of production
17 Second World War // WWII
18 25
19 14 tons/tonnes
20 (used in) Australia // used locally

Listening Section 3

21 human activity // humans
22 get warmer
23 influences
24 earth's temperature
25 (the) oceans
26 engines
27 (in) space, (in) orbit, above us/the Earth
28 B ⎫ in
29 C ⎬ any
30 E ⎭ order

Listening Section 4

31 developing countries
32 (large) African birds // (Mauritius) falcons
33 reptile house
34 animals
35 (the) English (language)
36 (animal) conservation
37 (zoo) keepers
38 (over) 350
39 Chinese student
40 (present) Conservation Officer

Academic Reading Section 1

1 B ⎫ in
2 D ⎬ any
3 E ⎭ order
4 rigs and/or tanks
5 fish stocks
6 physical obstacles
7 concrete
8 commercial
9 Japan
10 sea (grass) beds/floor/bottom
11 bamboo and coconuts
12 management (control)
13 C

Academic Reading Section 2

14 iii
15 vii

16 i
17 ix
18 vi
19 ii
20 NO
21 YES
22 YES
23 NOT GIVEN
24 NO
25 adolescents
26 1955
27 Virginia Slims

Academic Reading Section 3

28 C
29 D
30 B
31 B
32 A
33 D
34 E
35 doubled
36 dropped
37 less
38 no
39 slightly
40 reversed

General Training Reading Section 1

1 F
2 A
3 B
4 D
5 FALSE
6 NOT GIVEN
7 FALSE
8 FALSE
9 TRUE
10 vii
11 vi
12 ii
13 iii
14 iv

General Training Reading Section 2

15 A
16 C
17 TRUE
18 NOT GIVEN
19 TRUE

20 FALSE
21 D
22 E
23 H
24 A
25 B
26 H

General Training Reading Section 3

27 proportions
28 copies
29 varnish
30 transportation
31 composition
32 layer
33 sound
34 (auburn-red/rich) varnish
35 maple and spruce
36 minerals
37 £4
38 volcanic ash
39 their thickness
40 (a) perfect balance // a combination of factors

Assessing your results

Give yourself one point for each correct answer. Add up your scores out of 40 for Listening and Reading and look at the table on page 189 to see what IELTS band score you would have achieved.

IELTS Band Scores

Listening

Score	Band score
1	1
2 to 3	2
4 to 9	3
10 to 16	4
17 to 24	5
25 to 32	6
33 to 37	7
38 to 39	8
40	9

Academic Reading

Score	Band score
1	1
2 to 3	2
4 to 9	3
10 to 15	4
16 to 22	5
23 to 28	6
29 to 35	7
36 to 39	8
40	9

General Training Reading

Score	Band score
1 to 2	1
3 to 5	2
5 to 11	3
12 to 17	4
18 to 25	5
26 to 34	6
35 to 37	7
38 to 39	8
40	9

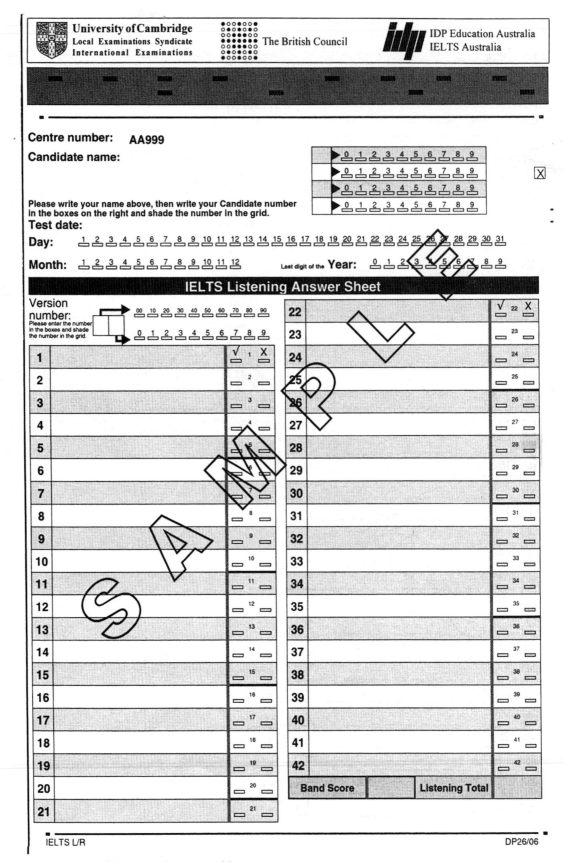

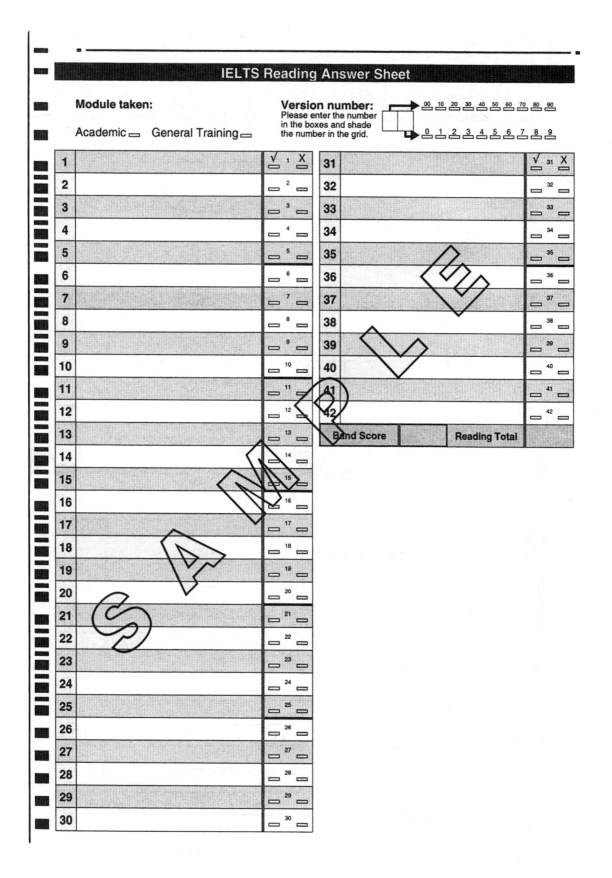

IELTS Reading Answer Sheet

Module taken:

Academic ⬜ General Training ⬜

Version number:
Please enter the number in the boxes and shade the number in the grid.

| 00 | 10 | 20 | 30 | 40 | 50 | 60 | 70 | 80 | 90 |
| 0 | 1 | 2 | 3 | 4 | 5 | 6 | 7 | 8 | 9 |

#		√ X
1		1
2		2
3		3
4		4
5		5
6		6
7		7
8		8
9		9
10		10
11		11
12		12
13		13
14		14
15		15
16		16
17		17
18		18
19		19
20		20
21		21
22		22
23		23
24		24
25		25
26		26
27		27
28		28
29		29
30		30

#		√ X
31		31
32		32
33		33
34		34
35		35
36		36
37		37
38		38
39		39
40		40
41		41
42		42

Band Score		Reading Total	

SAMPLE

Acknowledgements

The authors and publishers would like to thank the teachers and students who trialled and commented on the material:

Australia: Lynn Banbrook, Pauline Cullen, Carolyn Watts, Katie Dunworth; Greece: Annette Obee; Japan: Miles Craven; Malaysia: A. Sundram; Thailand: Dennis Derkenne, Bette Bowling, Paul Wallis; UK: Anthea Bazin, Jan Farndale, Don Hassett, Pat O'Sullivan, Carolyn Walker, Buddug Temple

The authors and publisher are grateful to the following for permission to use copyright material in *Insight into IELTS*. While every effort has been made, it has not been possible to identify the sources of all the material used and in such cases the publishers would welcome information from the copyright owners:

The *Geographical Magazine* for the extract on pp. 29–30 and 38 from 'The Dynamic Continent' by Adrian Fox and Janet Taylor, *The Geographical Magazine* Dec 1995, for the article on p. 49 'Penguins show signs of stress' by Frank Nowikowski, *The Geographical Magazine* October 1995 and for the extract on pp. 133–4 from 'Industrial Revolution' by Claire Hutchings, *The Geographical Magazine* May 1996; Sir John Houghton for the extract on p. 30 from 'Why we must be stewards of our soil', published in *The Independent*, 2 Mar 1996; *Independent Newspapers* for extracts a) and c) on p. 56 from 'When an elephant gets emotional' by Hugh Aldersley Williams; *Focus Magazine* for the extract on p. 31 from 'The undersea world of sound' by Peter Evans, *Focus* April 1995, for the extract on p. 34 from 'Sifting through the sands of time' by Carol Muskoron and Piers Alder, *Focus* July 1994, and for the extract on pp. 153–4 from '300-year-old secrets of Stradivarius' by Julian Brown, *Focus* July 1994; Curtis Brown on behalf of David Lodge for the extracts on pp. 32 and 53–54 from *The Practice of Writing* by David Lodge, published by Secker & Warburg, copyright © 1996; *The Times* for the extract on p. 35 from 'Divers speed hunt for ruins of Pharos lighthouse' by Christopher Walker from *The Times*, 21 July 1995, © Times Newspapers Limited 1995, and for the extract on p. 40 from 'Salty rice plant boosts harvests' by Sean Hargrave from *The Sunday Times*, 26 January 1997, © Times Newspapers Limited 1997 and for the extract on pp. 46–7 from 'Prehistoric insects spawn new drugs' by Steve Connor, *The Sunday Times*, 1 September 1996, © Times Newspapers Limited 1996 and for the diagram on p. 74, © John Smith/The Sunday Times, 1st June 1996; *BBC Wildlife Magazine* for the article on p. 37 'Baby Love' by Angela Turner, BBC Wildlife Magazine, March 1996; Robert Nurden for the extract on p. 65 from 'Visit to student fair is vital homework' published in *The European*, 20 March 1997; *Hallmark Editions* for the extract on pp. 44–5 from 'Australia's first commercial wind farm', published in GEO, vol. 17, no. 6, Nov/Dec 1995; *Runner's World* for the extracts on p. 61 from 'Six of the best rain jackets', *Runner's World* Dec 1995; *New Scientist* for the extract on p. 51 from 'Australia's growing disaster' by Ian Anderson, *New Scientist* 29 July 1995; Verdict Research Limited for graphs 12 a) and 12 c) on p. 71, © Verdict Research Limited 1998; The Policy Studies Institute, *University of Westminster Press* for the graph at the top of p. 74; *The Guardian* for the graph on p. 75 from *The Guardian*, 30 September 1997; Cambridge University Press for listening material in Unit 7, Extract 2, derived from *The Cambridge Encyclopedia of Langua*ge, © Cambridge University Press 1997; the exercise on pp. 151–2 is based on information that appeared in the program for the University of Sydney's Courses and Careers Day in 1997; Buderim Ginger for information used on pp. 129–30.

Gerrit Buntrock for p. 37. Christies Images for p. 153. Bruce Coleman Collection/Jens Rydell for p. 44. The Guardian/Jenny Ridley for p. 77. The Orion Publishing Group Ltd for p. 56. Tony Stone Images/ Chuck Davis for p. 31, /Stephen Frink for p. 133, /Howard Grey for p. 47, /Kevin Schafer for p. 49. Max Glaskin/The Sunday Times 1996 for p. 76. SYGMA/Jacques Delacour for p. 34. Telegraph Colour Library/John Lythgoe for p. 40. The photo of the artificial reef on p. 133 is © Southampton Oceanography Centre/Dr Anthony Jensen.

The photos on pp. 56 and 58 were taken on commission by Trevor Clifford, and those on pp. 7, 28, 66, 96, 100 and 103 by Gareth Boden and Rebecca Watson.

Illustrated by Kathy Baxendale: pp. 10, 79, 122, 126; Nick Duffy: pp. 14, 97; Gecko DTP: pp. 11, 20, 67, 68, 69, 70, 71, 72, 73, 74, 75, 76, 77, 144, 147; Amanda McPhail: Icons; Martin Sanders: pp. 24, 36, 156; Jamie Sneddon: pp. 12, 13, 22, 107, 115, 116, 117, 129, 146, 149, 151; Sam Thompson: pp. 8, 15, 127; Kath Walker: p. 17; Celia Witchard: p. 99.

Produced by Gecko Ltd

The cassette recording was produced by Martin Williamson at Studio AVP, London